THREE PLAYS
BY JEAN FINDLAY

Enemy Territory

A Phantom Lover

Little Black Raincloud

JEAN FINDLAY

Jean Findlay was born in Edinburgh, Scotland. She studied Law and French at Edinburgh University and Theatre in Krakow, Poland with Tadeusz Kantor. She ran a theatre company, writing and producing plays in Berlin, Bonn, Dublin, Rotterdam and the Pompidou Centre in Paris. She has written for the *Scotsman*, *Independent*, *Time Out* and the *Guardian* and is the author of *Chasing Lost Time – The life of CK Scott Moncrieff: Soldier, Spy and Translator* published by Chatto and Windus (2014) and Vintage paperbacks (2015) and Farrar, Straus and Giroux, New York (2015).

CONTENTS

Introduction	5
Enemy Territory	9
A Phantom Lover	79
Little Black Raincloud	125

To the Unknown Actress

Scotland Street Press
7/1 Scotland Street
Edinburgh EH3 6PP

Copyright © 2015 Jean Findlay
All rights reserved.

Jean Findlay has asserted her right to be identified as the author of this work
in accordance with the Copyright, Designs and Patents Act 1988

ISBN: 978-1-910895-01-6

Typeset by Palimpsest Book Production Limited, Falkirk, Stirlingshire
Printed in Scotland by Bell & Bain Limited, Glasgow

Jacket design by Theo Shack from a photograph by Philippe Fraser

INTRODUCTION

Enemy Territory was written during the conflict in the former Yugoslavia, about a visionary war victim. It had a reading with Ramin Gray from the Royal Court Theatre in London in 2000, with a stellar reading cast.

A Phantom Lover, set in present day Edinburgh and Cairo in 1943, had its first performance at the Bratsera on the Island of Hydra, Greece in 2002.

Little Black Raincloud, set in present-day London under threat of a terror strike, has yet to be performed.

In retrospect, these plays all have as a constant the theme of war: actual, remembered or threatened. I did not set out with this intention, as I have never experienced war at first hand, only read about it, seen reports, heard relatives talking about the Second World War, and felt occasionally a frisson of the threat. So I do not know why this theme exists: perhaps because war brings out the best and worst in us, extremes heighten human character, and we hear about conflict somewhere in the world on a daily basis. We all thirst for virtue: heroism, self-sacrifice and courage seen in action give us energy to fuel our lives. On the other side of the coin, we are also blood-thirsty and seekers of tragedy.

These plays are all tragi-comic.

The title of *Enemy Territory* comes from a line from the poet Stevie Smith, "Sometimes being alive is like living in enemy Territory". My sister died of a mental illness in 1994, and I realized that the terror, stress and agony she experienced in everyday life were akin to being in a war zone. The play's main character, Jenny, is both a war victim and a young woman in a mental hospital. She prays aloud to God in distress and her pleas get hooked into the wrong lines receiving replies from Socrates, Kierkegaard, a Rabbi, and an insurance salesman. These male voices from the top of history converse with a woman at the bottom of history – a pregnant housewife in a war zone, a mentally ill female. Her pure and courageous voice combats their authority, like St Joan or Alice.

A Phantom Lover is about the relationship between an 84–year-old lady and her young student cleaner. The old lady, Isobel, worked for the Special Operations Executive during the Second World War and Sally, her cleaner, reactivates memories from this time: memories so vivid that they walk on stage in the form of her now dead lover, Joseph. Edinburgh in the year 2000 becomes Cairo 1943 and Sally gets caught up in the action.

Little Black Raincloud involves no ghosts, but is about a young family living under the threat of a terrorist attack in London in 2006. Jess, who has a four-month-old baby,

~ INTRODUCTION ~

is married to a neurotic and depressed John. Their tense lives are brightened by the entry of Cathy, a friend and nurse, and Calum, Jess' brother who was a soldier. The radio announces that an "incident" has finally happened, the terrorist attack John has been fearing. In fact, the Four Horses of the Apocalypse are clattering down the platform at Paddington station. Surreal events prompt change in the lives of all four characters.

* * *

Plays previously produced include *The Big Tease* in 1992 at the Carlton Studios in Edinburgh and on tour to Die Lanterne in Rotterdam followed by *Call Me Susan* at the Traverse Theatre in Edinburgh in 1993. Neither of these plays were about war. The first was a devised play with strippers from the Edinburgh go-go bars and a choreographer from the Royal Shakespeare Company, Liz Rankin; an explosive cocktail of dance and rhetoric. The second, *Call Me Susan*, was a drama-documentary on stage about the practice of prostitution. It featured a Socratic dialogue between an old and a young whore, while waited on by the novelist Paul Sussman and serenaded by a tubist, John Desimone. Meanwhile a screen behind documented the actual lives and thoughts of prostitutes working in Krakow, Amsterdam, Paris, Edinburgh and Glasgow. These plays are not published but were well reviewed.

Telegraph: "Jean Findlay combines bruising emotional impact with infectious good humour."

Scotsman: "Resonant, moving and unmistakably real."

La Repubblica: "An intrepid and surefooted writer ... both Wildean and Platonic."

Edinburgh Evening News: "A cross between Dario Fo and Beckett, if he'd been a woman."

ENEMY TERRITORY

a play in two acts

by Jean Findlay

Characters

JENNY .... a pregnant woman, aged 30
SOCRATES .... abstracted but compassionate
KIERKEGAARD .... a nervy, frustrated type, obsessed by his own ideas
DR S .... a psychiatrist, played by same actor as Socrates
CLAIRE .... Jenny's sister
ROGER JOHNSON ..... a contemporary insurance salesman
RABBI .... Hassidic, mystical
DR COLEFAX .... a psychiatric doctor
GEORGE .... Jenny's husband
NURSE
1 AYLESBURY DUCK

The action takes place in the 1990s, partly in rural Central Europe (Hut) and partly in a mental hospital in London or Edinburgh (Hospital).

ACT ONE

SCENE ONE (HUT)

Jenny is kneeling on the floor of a three-sided wooden hut structure. One wall has been taken away to allow the audience to see in. Around the outside are bushes. The floor is covered in earth. It is flattened hard in the hut and looser outside. Jenny is wearing good but dirty clothes and is evidently about six months pregnant. She has the open, simple face of an unsophisticated person. She is a dignified character, played straight and sincere, not emotionally expressionistic.

JENNY: Out of the depths I cry to thee
O Lord, hear my prayer
May your ears be attentive to
The voice ... my voice ... I can't remember it

(*Despairing*) Dear God, please God, hear my prayer. All I want is for this war to end. No, that's not all I want, I want George, my husband. I miss him. Why can't I touch him when he's only a few miles away? Why can't I lie on his belly with my ear to his navel listening to his meal digesting? That's all I want, is that too much to ask you, Lord? It's not much. Some people pray for success and riches and to pass their exams and for new bicycles, and you sometimes even grant it.

I've seen it, in peacetime. All I want is normality – what do I get? This. It's not as if I asked for a palace and you gave me a hut – I don't mind about the hut – (*She hits a few walls*) – it's fine, as huts go. It's the enemy I don't like – the men (*Pained*). My mother always told me when in extremis, to pray. So I do. I stay here and pray. The other women escaped. (*Angry*) God, I do this every day and I never get a reply. Alright, humble now (*Kneels down*). Dear God, I know you are out there and that no matter what happens you are loving me. No matter what they do to me, how they humiliate me, I can rely on your presence – or absence as the case may be – sorry, did I say absence? I didn't mean to, it was him, distracting me.

Walking towards her through the bushes comes an elderly man with a white beard, dressed in a long, white linen gown tied at the waist with a cord. He is bare foot.

JENNY: (*Bewildered*) Hey … (*Suddenly very humbled*) God … ? Excuse me, God? Hello, is that you, God ?

SOCRATES: (*For it is he, stands for a while scratching his beard, ruminating. Eventually he says*) Xantippe, please be quiet.

JENNY: God? (*She is still on her knees*)

SOCRATES: The definition of piety; that which is beloved by the Gods, for the Gods, to the Gods; yet the gods are constantly at war, constantly fighting. (*Turns to Jenny*) Wish they'd stop, don't you?

JENNY: I wish they'd drown themselves.

SOCRATES: Well, that wouldn't help much would it? They are after all at home fighting, quarrelling, disputing territory. That's why Mount Olympus is in Cyprus. Gods have the same petty jealousies as us, only more glamour and fame, and that's what turns them into monsters. The problem of perception is to know which side of the camera you are on. The gods are always on both.

All this time Jenny is staring at Socrates.

SOCRATES: (*Annoyed*) What are you doing?

JENNY: Looking at you.

SOCRATES: Well stop looking at me. Where was I …? Oh yes, perception and reality – I never

	used these terms as much as they do today. I'm more interested in the definition of piety, really. You (*turning to Jenny*) inspired that thought – asking if I was a god. Do you love the gods?
JENNY:	There is only one God.
SOCRATES:	Well, what if there were more? Say 37, all sitting up there eating ambrosia and sipping nectar. Piety would mean more – that you had to love all of them, implore all of them for help and wisdom, steadfastness, stability and wit …
JENNY:	(*Giggles*) Has anyone ever told you that you are barmy?
SOCRATES:	Many people. But then I provide entertainment for people in pain. You are in pain, I can see that. But no, I'm not God … I can't help you … I can't touch you.
JENNY:	(*Coming forward*) Yes, you can. (*Reaches out*) Try.
SOCRATES:	(*Stepping back*) Even I have fear. You know I fought in the Punic Wars, a foot soldier, recommended for bravery; that's courage in

the outer world. Courage in the inner world is different. You bear the scars of war in your eyes ... and here (*hand on stomach*) but I can't help you with your pain ...

JENNY: (*Suddenly hurt*) I don't want you to, thank you. That's not what I'm asking. (*Turns away, hugging herself*)

SOCRATES: (*Scratching his head distractedly and making his white hair stand on end*) Yes?

JENNY: Who are you anyway?

SOCRATES: Socrates. I'm a teacher.

JENNY: What do you teach?

SOCRATES: Thought. What do you do?

JENNY: (*Her face set*) I am kept, by the soldiers.

SOCRATES: (*Ashamed*) I know that, but before ... before the war.

JENNY: It's difficult to imagine. I was just married to George. We'd saved up for ages. We didn't have children immediately, we had time to read. He joined up when the war came and

>   was sent away ... but I'm ... waiting for ...
>   George to come. I'm pregnant as well ...

SOCRATES: With the child of the enemy.

JENNY: Yes.

SOCRATES: And you think George will come?

JENNY: I pray for that every day.

Socrates is both ashamed and impressed. He puts his hand into his pocket and pulls out a large onion.

SOCRATES: I'm afraid this is all I have to give you. (*He bends cautiously, almost with reverence and rolls the onion towards her.*)

JENNY: (*Watches it stop at her feet*) No, it's not. You can help me – you can teach me thought.

SOCRATES: (*Muses a bit*) Let's see. A definition of war? (*Sees the reaction of hurt sadness on Jenny's face*) No, here it would send you round the bend. Faith is cleaner, more powerful. Stick with that. I must get on.

JENNY: Wait, what do you mean? (*Holds his gown*)

SOCRATES: Faith and reason, an old debate. With faith you can leap straight onto the lap of the gods – it's like pure mathematics. Whereas reason, like arithmetic, is a slower, plodding, more tortuous path, you may never get there. But for some reason, it's far more respectable.

JENNY: Reason, for some reason, is more respectable. What reason? Can't you see? I need to know.

SOCRATES: (*Sighing*) It's a long and complicated reason. And I really must go.

JENNY: Don't go, I get so lonely. Please teach me thought.

SOCRATES: (*Hesitating*) Is the war the same for you as it is for the soldier?

JENNY: No. (*She picks up the onion and begins to peel it quickly, taking one skin off after the other.*) This isn't the same for the onion is it? (*She continues until the tears are rolling down her cheeks*) We used to keep ducks – they'd get all dirty around their necks in the mud and they couldn't get clean. If they aren't clean they can't keep warm because their feathers are too bedraggled. Then if they can't keep warm they just die. They are so frail. Just dirt can kill them, and cold. But if they can get water and clean themselves then the feathers are fluffy again. You should see the way they preen themselves. Very efficiently, almost violent with their snouts, and they mutter all the time. I wish I had one to keep me company. (*Sobbing*)You think I'm being irrational don't you?

Socrates leaves stage left.

SCENE TWO (HUT)

A man in 19th-century Danish town clothes with purple velveteen breeches enters stage right. He is carrying an Aylesbury duck under his arm.

KIERKEGAARD: No, not irrational. The irrational mind produces faeries and spirits, the rational mind creates philosophers and that's much more dangerous. Here, take this. (*He puts the duck down in the hut.*)
Now stop crying. I thought you wanted a duck.

JENNY: I do, for company, thank you very much. (*She strokes the duck and tries to feed it some of the onion, which it refuses.*)
Who are you?

KIERKEGAARD: Kierkegaard. Stop crying; despair is a sin.

JENNY: (*Wiping her eyes*) Sometimes I find being me very hard to bear. Are you a thinker?

KIERKEGAARD: I suppose so.

JENNY: Why?

KIERKEGAARD: Why? Why? Why? To escape, that's why. A thinker, as opposed to a doer. I had a difficult life too. Didn't have the guts to get married. My father was a tyrant; he kicked his first wife to death. I'm a Protestant you know. Sins of the forefathers. I was afraid I would have kicked Regina to death.

JENNY: Who's Regina?

KIERKEGAARD: My fiancée. I'd have nagged her, or wanted her to fulfil some impossible metaphysical expectation. She wouldn't have been happy. She couldn't have had that simple bliss, that beatific grace that is the right of all women, all women who love and have children. You know those Renaissance paintings, that calm voluptuous look – (*Turning to Jenny*) – You have it almost. She'd never have had that, not with me.

JENNY: Why not?

KIERKEGAARD: Can you imagine a Christian marriage with all that it entails? If you live according to your word at the ceremony, your duty, love, energy, is to your wife to make her happy, and who can ever make a woman happy? Not that she was the frivolous, whimsical type, oh no, Regina was Athene in all her splendour: devout, wise, obedient, charming, self-contained, ethereal almost. She'd never have demanded anything – and then I'd never have given her anything, I'd have made her life a misery. And I couldn't have got a proper paying job. Can you imagine me as a banker? I am only beginning to explore the approach to Christianity; to the thought of it.

JENNY: So you never got married?

KIERKEGAARD: It was against my vocation as a radical thinker.

JENNY: You should never have thought so much about it. It's not about thought. It's about love.

KIERKEGAARD: Are you married?

JENNY: Yes. My husband is called George, he's a soldier now.

KIERKEGAARD: You are with child.

JENNY: It's not his.

KIERKEGAARD: I'm sorry.

JENNY: That's the way things are. I'm a victim of circumstance.

KIERKEGAARD: Perhaps that's better than being a victim of thought. At least you've got a child, all I have is a pile of bloody books that no one will print. They hate me, they jibe and lampoon me, they ...

JENNY: I was raped.

KIERKEGAARD: Oh ... (*Thinks for a while*) "You shall have a life scorned by other girls, you will be treated as a giddy and conceited hussy, or a poor half-mad wretch, or a wanton woman, etc., and you will also be exposed to every possible kind of suffering, and at the end a sword will pierce through your soul (Luke 2.35) when you see that God himself will seem to have abandoned you. And this is the glad news! Yes, all honour to her that without hesitating a moment could say 'Behold the handmaid of the Lord'" ...

JENNY: But I didn't say "Behold the handmaid of the Lord."

KIERKEGAARD: But, don't you see? You're the perfect Christian! The Saviour of the world lives in poverty and humility, then is persecuted and hated, finally is tortured in every way and crucified.

JENNY: But I don't want to be crucified.

KIERKEGAARD: You are much more of a Christian than I am. I was born into so-called Christendom, where my whole life from the earliest was crammed full of the trickery that turns Christianity into optimism, bland optimism.

JENNY: Well, we don't have that problem anymore. We don't have Christendom. But life can still be pretty bland.

KIERKEGAARD: Your life isn't bland.

JENNY: There is something to be said for blandness occasionally.

KIERKEGAARD: (*Indignant again*) Do you know what they call me? "The first existentialist".

JENNY: What's an existentialist?

KIERKEGAARD: One of these black-clothed types with a

	goatee who sit around French universities contemplating suicide. I never contemplated suicide.
JENNY:	I do.
KIERKEGAARD:	Well, you shouldn't. Despair is a sin
JENNY:	No, it's not. Christ despaired on the cross, it's well documented.
KIERKEGAARD:	So, just because he did, it doesn't mean it's not a sin, not everything he did was right. He was half-human, you know.
JENNY:	You make him sound like a minotaur.
KIERKEGAARD:	Anyway you're not on a cross.
JENNY:	How do you know? You started out by saying I was the perfect Christian. Look just tell me. Did Christ ever make any jokes? Even one? In all those books of the Bible is there even one piece of humour?
KIERKEGAARD:	I wouldn't know ... that's an idea. I'm a bit of free-thinker myself. But despair is a sin.
JENNY:	Please explain.

KIERKEGAARD: Thought is a creative process. The actions you think of you will one day do – the world you create you will one day enter.

JENNY: At least my world is entertaining. Jokes are what stop you despairing, nothing else.

KIERKEGAARD: I'm sorry, I don't know any.

JENNY: Who do you think tells me jokes then? In here?

KIERKEGAARD: I don't know, the other women?

JENNY: They all escaped, I'm alone in this hut. No, it's God who tells me the jokes.

KIERKEGAARD: (*Surprised*) Perhaps you could share a few with me. I might be able to perk up some of my pamphlets.

JENNY: You wouldn't understand the humour – it's an acquired taste.

KIERKEGAARD: Well, we are uppity.

JENNY: I'm not.

KIERKEGAARD: What?

JENNY:	Uppity. That was a heartless thing to say.
KIERKEGAARD:	Well, you wouldn't tell me the joke. You're very well educated.
JENNY:	I had a good teacher, the best some might say.
KIERKEGAARD:	Who?
JENNY:	Socrates.
KIERKEGAARD:	Now, you're joking.
JENNY:	He was here before you arrived. But he couldn't help me.
KIRKEGAAARD:	Why do you need help?
JENNY:	My life is sad, cruel and empty.
KIERKEGAARD:	Whose isn't? What do you want me to do? Get out the violins? No, really, there are cogitative cures for sadness. Think of the good things in life, brown paper packages tied up with string, that sort of line. Look, I wanted to break out of that depraved cycle, birth, pain, marriage, pain, birth, pain … I wanted to thrust the power

	of my thought into eternity and that's what I did; so that I would live when others died. The pain and the pleasure of my thought, the ecstasy of the mind, how much greater than the ecstasy of the body!
JENNY:	And the pain of the body?
KIERKEGAARD:	Oh, that just kills you, but the pain of the mind, if you're strong, if you know what you're doing – you can circumnavigate madness.

Kierkegaard exits majestically. Jenny is alone.

JENNY:	But that world is only frightening when you can't control it – when you're tired, mainly. It's because George isn't here. I don't like being left on my own without love around me – mature, responsible, selfless love. That's why we need to feel the love of God. I try and I try and I get hooked into the wrong lines. I get some philosopher, or someone who can't love, who can only think. (*Pause*) Weakness, one's own weakness, is frightening.

SCENE THREE (HOSPITAL)

The lighting eliminates Jenny and her hut and to the right sits Dr S, an elderly man at a desk covered in papers and books. He is played by the same actor as Socrates, but his beard and hair are tidy and his clothes are contemporary. Opposite him on the edge of her seat sits a young woman who looks like Jenny, except that she too is tidier. She could be a school-teacher. She is in fact Jenny's sister Claire.

CLAIRE:	You're the only person I could think of who might be able to help Jenny, Doctor.
DR S:	My dear Claire, you know I was forcibly retired years ago. They don't listen to me anymore; they think I'm a hairy maverick. I have no influence on the wards.
CLAIRE:	But you have a lifetime's experience – all your books …
DR S:	I may be able to help *you*. What do you want to know?
CLAIRE:	I want to know what's going on in her mind. She's my sister but she doesn't know me; she stares into space for hours, and

comes round with a terrible headache. She mutters about war and philosophy; she wants to read Plato, but she can't even change her clothes – they're filthy.

DR S: (*Turning over some papers*) It says here …

CLAIRE: (*Jumping up, pleased*) You've got her notes … She can't stand her doctor.

DR S: I did manage to acquire them. Dr Colefax … hmm … his bedside manner is notoriously lacking in empathy – but technically he's a good doctor, you can't fault him. He's given a diagnosis of manic depression … and … (*He reads in silence then looks up*) … I'd say she's having a series of organized hallucinations, brought about by shock. You told me of the death of her husband. How did he die?

CLAIRE: The first British soldier to die in the war in Central Europe – a sniper got him they hushed it up of course. He was always in the army. He was in the army when she married him. I suppose you must consider that risk. I did say that. I did try to help.

DR S: I'm sure you did. She's also pregnant. There are some notes about rape.

CLAIRE: The child's not George's.

DR S: Was she raped?

CLAIRE: I'm not sure. After he died, she was so mad with grief, so desperate for comfort ...

DR S: You don't know who the father is.

CLAIRE: It could've been anyone. She spent a fortnight in Paris. I shouldn't have lent her the money. I thought a holiday would distract her. Perhaps it *was* rape.

DR S: But she's not happy with her pregnancy.

CLAIRE: No ...Yes ... She does want to have the baby. It's the idea of rape. You see it's more complicated. She spends every day examining the newspaper reports from the war in Central Europe – saying we can't imagine the horror, and she can, she can almost experience it. There are so many articles about rape ...

DR S: Aha ... (*Stands up, paces*) You must take her seriously, Claire. She is at war. When we experience such phenomenal highs and lows, we do hang life and death in the balance. The spectrum of ideas and emotions in a manic-depressive is too much for the human mind. It distorts and exaggerates to an extent we as "normal" people can barely understand. There *is* a battle going on inside Jenny: a battle between life and death, the real and the imaginary. If we have a good imagination, it can very often seem more appealing than actual life. The reason you must take this battle seriously, Claire, is that fifteen per cent of manic-depressives take their own lives.

CLAIRE: But I can't cope with her, really, I can't. Isn't hospital the best place? I've done the best thing, haven't I?

DR S: If you can't cope, there is no better place – if she gets the right person and the right treatment.

CLAIRE: ... and if she doesn't ...

DR S: Sometimes the medical professions fail because they are clumsy. "Science without religion is lame. Religion without science is blind." Who said that?

CLAIRE: I don't know ... Socrates?

DR S:	No, Einstein. What I mean is that you need to have a mixture of humanity and medical knowledge – and be strong on both – in order to deal with manic depression.
CLAIRE:	Why can't you treat her?
DR S:	She's under section – I'm afraid she's in the hands of the hospital.
CLAIRE:	Surely fifteen per cent is not that high a percentage; it's like the possibility of a car accident, isn't it?
DR S:	Nnnnnot quite. You wouldn't for example be able to take out life insurance for her.

This scene disappears completely and light comes up on Jenny in her hut.

SCENE FOUR (JENNY'S HUT)

Enter a large desk on wheels pushed by Roger, an insurance salesman in a suit, white shirt, whorly silk tie, and highly polished shoes. His hair is slightly oily. Roger sits in various positions on and around the desk while manipulating the phone and his large diary. He is constantly active and talkative and turns to Jenny by way of explanation.

ROGER: I'm trying to get Adam ... Hello, hello ... is that Mr Smith? Mr Smith, I got your telephone number from a student of yours who said that you were in financial difficulty. Now, I am part of a large group of financial consultants and am here to help. Mr Smith ... may I call you Adam? ... No (*smiling*) you're not Eve ... no, no, I'm not. She was genuinely concerned about you and knew I would offer to help. A doctor for physical problems, a psychiatrist for mental problems and Future Finances for your money problems. What do you mean you've never heard of a psychiatrist ... this is the twentieth century ... What? ... He's put the phone down.

JENNY: What's the hurry?

ROGER: (*Ignoring her, straightening his tie and the diary*) Keep focused. (*Redials*) Hello. Mr Smith? I'm afraid we got cut off. You forgot to tell me your occupation ... I'm Roger, Roger Johnson ... financial consultant ... Well, I know that teachers don't earn much money, but if you save wisely, and invest properly, you can enjoy your retirement. How does the idea of an impoverished old age grab you? Not being able to afford heating bills, medical bills, not eating properly? All your teeth fall out. Are you scared of that? Quite right too, I would be. But I have put my money into Bumper Bonds and Super Pension Plus Plans. Now the thing about BBs and SPPPs is that, unlike jobs, they last. They are the imaginary end of the finance world, we create them, you buy them, and they exist. Very simple, it's like God, a simple correlation between creation and existence ... Hello, hello?

(*Puts phone down*)

JENNY: You shouldn't try and sell people God. They will think you are a Mormon.

ROGER: I wasn't selling God, I'm selling insurance, (*exasperated*) I don't know what's wrong ...

	I usually use sports analogies. Who are you anyway?
JENNY:	Jenny.
ROGER:	Roger. Hi. What are you doing here?
JENNY:	I live here.
ROGER:	Right … (*Inspects hut*) Do you have a pension plan?
JENNY:	(*Looks baffled*)
ROGER:	A stash of money to ensure you are not impoverished in your old age. What you do is you put by a bit each month, give it to me, I stuff it in a sock and give it back to you when you're 65, except it's grown by then, a giant sock, all stuffed with money. Think of it.
JENNY:	You *are* like a Mormon.
ROGER:	(*Laughing and sitting seductively on the edge of his desk*) How about life insurance?
JENNY:	How about it?

ROGER: Well, when you die, your loved ones, that child you're going to have, don't just experience loss – and extra expense; cost of funeral, wake, etcetera. But with insurance they get a load of money as well, it helps pay for the expenses and pours balm on troubled waters. In fact some customers are so satisfied with the insurance they say they don't experience any loss at all.

JENNY: What about me?

ROGER: Well we're talking about after your death. No, Jenny. It's you I'm interested in. Your loved ones, your goals. What are your goals in life?

JENNY: Goals.

ROGER: Things you aim for. Football language.

JENNY: I want my husband back.

ROGER: Ditch you, did he? Go off with another woman?

JENNY: No. No.

ROGER: I know, its hard to swallow. Best forget

	about him, though, there's loads of men out there. Not all for you perhaps, not every man will take on someone else's kid ... I'd have to think hard about it myself.
JENNY:	Shut up.
ROGER:	Hey.
JENNY:	I said shut up.
ROGER:	I'm only trying to help. It's you I'm interested in. I know it's hard. Been given the cold-shoulder myself a few times.
JENNY:	He's a soldier. He's fighting. And he's going to come and rescue me.
ROGER:	Right. And what are you doing to attain that goal?
JENNY:	I pray.
ROGER:	(*Turning to audience and rolling his eyes.*) You pray?
JENNY:	Not much else you can do in my condition.
ROGER:	You could try tap dancing. (*Quickly*) Just a

	joke. Look I'm a nice guy, nice people work in insurance. It gives you peace of mind. It really does.
JENNY:	Nice people probably worked for the Third Reich.
ROGER:	Now let's not get historical – that's not your problem – your problem is right here, your life, now. What about the kid?
JENNY:	It's not mine.
ROGER:	It's in your stomach.
JENNY:	I mean it's not my husband's, I was raped.
ROGER:	(*Genuinely shocked, gasps*) A girl like you? Not much you can do about that … terminate it. You have to. You'd be funny about it if you had it.

Telephone rings. Roger waits for it to ring twice.

ROGER: Future Finances … Call me Roger, I'll call you Adam … you'd prefer … OK Mr Smith. I just want to say that … what..? (*Face screws up*) You want me to tell them that? … Yes … yes … OK … (*Looks at audience*)

Mr Smith says that he influenced Marx just as much as he influenced Thatcher, and it's not his fault that a bunch of greasy insurance salesmen are pushing pensions down your throat ... (*back to Smith*) Hang on there. Listen nothing's your fault, baby. I know, we're not popular, us insurance salesmen, we get criticism from all sides, but we're providing a service people actually want. Demand and supply ... heard of it? ... What d'you mean you invented it? ... (*To audience ironically*) This man invented demand and supply. And how much did you get for that invention? The price of a lecture, and what's that? ... How many loaves of bread? ... Not much is it for the invention of demand and supply. History's made a better profit. What I want to say to you, Mr Smith, is this. Have you got a pension plan? That's a lot more important than the vagaries and accidents of history ... You know why most people aren't rich? Cos they don't want to be. That could be your problem. Too much thought and too little action. He's put the phone down again. Just as we were beginning to converse. (*Pause. Thinks.*) I was just about to have a conversation with a great man, there.

JENNY: (*Approaching him*) What do you mean, terminate it?

ROGER: Oh, you're still here.

JENNY: Yes, there's me and the phone.

ROGER: I was talking about your kid. None of my business I suppose, but I'd recommend an abortion.

JENNY: You're right, it is none of your business. (*Gesturing*) Why don't you take your desk, your tie, your telephone and get out.

Exit Roger pushing desk.

Jenny breathes a sigh of relief and gets down on her knees again.

JENNY: Thanks God, I could have done without him. Why can't you send me someone who understands ?

SCENE FIVE (HUT)

The sound of Klezmer music. Enter an Hassidic Rabbi, dancing. He has black ringlets, a beard, a hat, knee breeches and a long black coat. It is not possible to tell from which era he comes, because their garb has not changed since the 17th century. He dances lightly round the stage completely absorbed in his trance and stops still looking around, then shakes his head as if to break out of his trance. He is most courteous.

RABBI:	Excuse me, I don't usually come to places like this. This is not heaven. Prosce pani, I beg your pardon madam. I'm very sorry.
JENNY:	About what?
RABBI:	I didn't mean to disturb you.
JENNY:	I'm used to it by now. If you were looking for heaven, you must have got the wrong door.
RABBI:	I wasn't looking for a door. Anyway it doesn't work like that.

The Klezmer music starts quietly and the Rabbi begins to dance again.

JENNY: Please don't go.

RABBI: You did call me, then.

JENNY: Yes, except that I didn't know it was you.

RABBI: That's alright, I understand, it often happens. You can tell me your troubles.

JENNY: If only I could express them, tell them all … (*Starts to cry*) … I can't stop crying … (*Continues crying*)

RABBI: You know there is a sea of human tears. Tears of sorrow, of hidden aspirations, of broken hearts.

JENNY: I'm sure. Some are mine. (*Still crying*).

RABBI Let me tell you a story. (*Sits down*) After Adam and Eve had been banished from the Garden of Eden, God saw they were penitent and said to them, "Unfortunate children, you have now been driven from the garden where you living with great well-being and without much care. Now you are about to enter a world of sorrow and trouble, the like of which staggers the imagination. However I want you to know that my benevolence and love for you will never end. I know that you will meet with much tribulation and it will embitter your lives. For this reason, I give you out of my treasure this priceless pearl. Look! It is a tear! And when grief overtakes you and your heart aches so that you are not able to endure it, then a tear will fall from your eyes. Your burden will grow lighter then." When Adam and Eve heard these words, sorrow overcame them. Tears welled up in their eyes, rolled down their cheeks and fell to earth. And it was these tears of anguish that first moistened the earth. Adam and Eve left them as an inheritance to their children. And since then, whenever a human being is in great trouble and his heart aches and his spirit is oppressed, the tears begin to flow from his eyes. And the gloom is lifted.

JENNY: That's a nice story. (*Pause*). But it's not much compensation really – to lose Paradise and gain a tear.

RABBI: Compensation is a very 20th-century concept.

JENNY: So I've been told. At least they had each other.

RABBI: Who?

JENNY: Adam and Eve. It's important. I could bear anything if I had George here.

RABBI: Of course. (*He rises, the Klezmer music starts and he begins to dance away*)

JENNY: The conversation inside your head is only that, it bears no relation to what you say out there. When it does, if it ever works, it is the strongest thing. What appears in your head is what you have nearer to God.

RABBI: Excuse me, I didn't mean to interrupt you. I thought you were finished.

JENNY: I was just thinking out loud.

RABBI: There is some truth in what you say. Remember what you say can be powerful, what you think can be powerful. The world you think up you may one day create. Remember you are in charge.

JENNY: It works if I close my eyes. (*Closes eyes and lies in foetal position*) I see George. Yes, his arms are around me and his hand is across my face. He likes to stroke my cheekbones

	and smooth my hair back. I kiss the hollow of his elbow and beneath his wrist. I want to kiss his eyes. I like the way he grips the small of my back.
RABBI:	And your child?
JENNY:	It's not his, but I'm going to keep it. I have to. It's part of the peace effort. You're the only person who's going to understand this, so I'll tell you. They are killing, so I'm not going to kill. Don't you understand? I'm not going to terminate it. This is the only antidote. This is life, they are death. This (*stomach*) is another human being. The conception was a shame, but the life of this child won't be. It will grow in love. The battle scars in this world are terrible; they come from an outburst of hatred. To heal them we must …
RABBI:	Love your enemies and pray for those who persecute you. It's the only answer, otherwise there's just wars all round.
JENNY:	That's just what I was going to say …
RABBI:	May I wish you luck in your encounters; remember always that God holds you in

the palm of his hand; trust and do not fear; if you fear you can create your worst fears. Good-bye.

The music starts again and the Rabbi dances away.

JENNY: The only thing I really fear is staying in hospital and having to face Dr Colefax.

SCENE SIX (HUT)

Enter a man in a white coat with a neat salt-and-pepper beard and round glasses. He is carrying a clipboard and speaks in clipped tones. He is Dr Colefax, a psychiatric doctor. He starts sane and lucid and gets progressively manic as the scene unfolds.

JENNY: God?

DR COLEFAX: No, but I've often been mistaken for a father figure.(*Looks at clipboard*) Post traumatic shock syndrome. You've been hearing voices … who've we got? (*Looks at clipboard*) Socrates, Kierkegaard, Napoleon – no, that's ward three – some pop star … Have you been hearing voices?

JENNY: I can hear your voice.

DR COLEFAX: Are these voices controllable by the conscious mind? Or are you out of control? Can you predict the actions and speech of these hallucinations?

JENNY: No, I wish I could.

DR COLEFAX: Hmmm. And you talk to God?

JENNY: I pray.

DR COLEFAX: Yes. Tell me, what do you "pray" about?

JENNY: None of your business.

DR COLEFAX: If you cooperate, we will make sure you are passed onto best health authorities on the non-urgent procedure initiatives to clear them from the waiting lines to someone with more purchasing power than a fund-holding practising general.

JENNY: I'm fine thank you, I don't need a health authority. I have my husband.

DR COLEFAX: Well, I can't see him.

JENNY: You wouldn't. Do you believe in the survival of the human personality after death?

DR COLEFAX: No. This life is all we have – which is why we are trying to treat you. You have to get well and get out of here. At the moment you're not very well. Listen, do yourself a favour, stop talking about God will you? Nobody's interested in God any more. It just makes people cringe. It's passé. What's worse is it makes people think you're

	madder than you really are. Especially conversation with God.
JENNY:	On the contrary, it's natural to talk to God, like a flower turning to the sun …
DR COLEFAX:	Whimsy!
JENNY:	Kierkegaard …
DR COLEFAX:	Kierkegaard! No one's interested in him anymore either. Now, if you discussed Adorno …
JENNY:	… I'd be as mad as you.
DR COLEFAX:	What am I supposed to do with that comment?
JENNY:	Slot it in somewhere in the vast gap you have between thought and feeling.
DR COLEFAX:	I'm your doctor, please show me some respect. I'm a learned man. I've read practically everything; literature, poetry, economics, medical science, phenomenology …
JENNY:	That means nothing. People eat gourmet

food and very often all that comes out is faeces.

DR COLEFAX: Now, let's discuss things nicely.

JENNY: You start.

DR COLEFAX: You're a very attractive woman …

JENNY: Do you know that's what the father of this child said. Then he got up, in a businesslike way and said, "That was good sex, thank you." In French of course.

DR COLEFAX: Of course.

JENNY: He said thank you, zipped himself up, wiped his nose with the back of his hand and left.

DR COLEFAX: Ergo, all men are rapists, or at least I'm a potential rapist.

JENNY: "Ergo". (*Laughs*) You're so pretentious.

DR COLEFAX: Pretentious? That won't get you anywhere. You've been seeing Kierkegaard! According to my brief you are subject to irrational beliefs: you think you've been raped, you're

	waiting for some husband, and are seeing Adam Smith ...
JENNY:	It wasn't Adam Smith. It was an insurance salesman trying to sell Adam Smith a pension plan by telephone.
DR COLEFAX:	(*Professionally*) Precisely ... (*Looks at notes*) Elvis?
JENNY:	No.
DR COLEFAX:	And a duck. Just tell me one thing ... Why the duck?
JENNY:	The duck's here. (*It is*)
DR COLEFAX:	Now look, let's be sensible about this. We'll hand you over to a fund-raising non-governmental organisation such as a fun family doctor-general, and then a mortician. That's part of the fun.
JENNY:	Who has the fun?
DOCTOR:	Whoever has the funds. But you must leave all that to the experts. You are safe in the hands of the experts. Now let's just give you a quick abortion.

Exit Dr Colefax and re-enter immediately pulling a sucker-type vacuum cleaner. It is on and sucking loudly. Jenny switches it off with her foot.

JENNY: If you must use it, then clean the floor. Please sit down. (*Colefax sits down.*) Allow me to explain something. Imagine there are two buckets of knowledge. In fact (*Jenny goes and gets two buckets from backstage*) you don't have to imagine. These are two buckets of knowledge.

COLEFAX: (*Peering cautiously into one of them*) Someone's been sick in this one.

JENNY: There are two buckets of knowledge: A and B. A represents my brain, and B yours. Notice they are the same size. The difference is in the contents. B is a stranger to the contents of bucket A and vice versa. The contents of bucket A are leaping around in a more excited manner than the contents of B. In fact they are so agitated that they are upsetting the balance of the whole bucket. The only way B can help is through imagination and empathy. B is an expert; he does not have imagination. What B does is pour in cement. The contents of A struggle hard and painfully to agitate. Pain is expressed, distress. B keeps on pouring in cement. Soon we won't be able to hear even the pain and the distress.

(All the while she is miming and illustrating and agitating the buckets)

It's simply disrespect. You won't heal anyone unless you have respect for their dignity.

DR COLEFAX: You are a simple woman, too easily swayed by sentiment.

JENNY: You are a clever man too good at masking feeling.

DR COLEFAX: You act on your emotions, why don't you move up a register.

JENNY: To what? Mind, intellect, spirit, soul, brain, belief system, will, courage, driving-force, libido, principle, life force, love, faith, generosity, courage, loyalty, wit, humility …

DR COLEFAX: Is humility your driving force? (*Laughs triumphantly*) It is isn't it?

JENNY: You don't know about humility, do you? Can you kneel? (*Pause*) Can you kneel?

Reluctantly Dr Colefax kneels.

JENNY : (*Standing over him quietly*) Unfortunately Dr Colefax, we are in a war zone. This is Central Europe. You are the illusion, I the reality.

Dr Colefax dissolves in a puff of black smoke. There is the noise of machine-gun fire, the flash and flare of bombs. War noises. Fighting. Jenny stands still. She is not frightened.

A man enters from the back of the theatre behind the audience wearing army flak gear, a wound on one arm and a bloody bandage around his head. He rushes towards the stage and violently picks Jenny up. They turn to face the audience. We have soft and normal lighting. It is not the enemy, but her husband, George. They embrace for some time.

GEORGE: Jenny, my love. Let's get out of here.

JENNY: Take the duck, she's my friend.

George picks Jenny up again. They leave with the duck following.

End of Act One

There is no interval, only darkness for scene change.

ACT TWO

SCENE ONE (HOSPITAL)

A white cell. All traces of mud and hut are gone. Sound of birdsong and a babbling brook. Jenny wakes from a hospital bed. She is more pregnant.

JENNY: George, George, GEORGE! (*To audience, rising*) Well, that didn't happen, did it? It was all a dream as they say. Listen, can you hear that? That's a dream. And you know what happens to dreams. They get stamped (*Stamps foot and out goes birdsong*) out (*Stamps foot again and out goes the sound of the brook*). Here they do. There's no place for dreams, conditions are too harsh, and those who dream in harsh conditions use their energy in dream not in survival. Dream is a luxury. Hah! George, George!

She starts to bash the walls. A nurse enters and holds her kindly.

NURSE: Would you like some water?

JENNY: Where's George?

NURSE: Jenny, you know he's not here, he was killed.

JENNY:	(*Crying*) But he came in, I saw him. He was there, just where you are. He took me in his arms.
NURSE:	No, dear. Calm yourself. Don't upset yourself.
JENNY:	(*To audience*) You saw him didn't you? You did, didn't you. (*She moves forward centre stage and challenges someone in the audience*) You saw him. (*Points*) He saw him.
NURSE:	There's no one here, dear. It's alright, it's alright, he won't come again.

Exit Nurse

SCENE TWO

George enters in normal clothes. He sits on the bed. Jenny is at once calm and serene. They look at each other and smile. There is a knock on the door and George gets under the bed as the nurse re-enters with a glass.

NURSE: Drink this, dear, you mustn't get too worked up.

Jenny takes it and lies back. Nurse rearranges the bedding and exits. Jenny sits up and squirts the mixture from her mouth back into the glass. George emerges from under the bed.

JENNY: They try and muffle nature because they are afraid of it.

GEORGE: I've got to get you out of here.

JENNY: I can't walk far you know. I couldn't squeeze out of a window. I can't jump. I'm so tired. I just want to rest. I keep losing it.

GEORGE: Are you in pain?

JENNY: Not physical.

George kisses her.

JENNY: Healed by the sweet coolness of his lips. It's so exhausting. You've no idea how exhausting it is.

GEORGE: Why don't you go to sleep just now. I'll be back.

JENNY: (*Drowsily*) Will you?

GEORGE: I have to get something.

She falls asleep holding his hand. George exits.

SCENE THREE

Nurse enters. She sits at a table to front right and starts to fill in forms.

NURSE: (*Muttering*) Female, thirty, relatives, sister, blood, O positive, thirty-six weeks, termination, category ...

JENNY: (*Waking*) Did you say termination?

NURSE: It's the best option.

JENNY: Best?

NURSE: When you have been detained under Section III of the Mental Healthy Act ...

JENNY: I have George ...

NURSE: We haven't been able to contact him.

JENNY: I've seen him.

NURSE: I know, dear – but as he hasn't contacted us, we must leave it to the doctors and social workers.

JENNY: Do I have no rights?

NURSE: You can challenge the section in a court of law, if you can organize it. You are entitled to representation.

JENNY: I'm so exhausted. You've no idea how exhausting it all is.

NURSE: That'll be the medication. It will give you rest and help you keep calm. It will do you good in the long term.

JENNY: But it takes such an effort to think straight. How can I organize a court case?

NURSE: We understand that.

JENNY: Perhaps George will help.

NURSE: (*Returning to paperwork*) Perhaps.

The Nurse finishes the admin while Jenny dozes. Nurse exits.

SCENE FOUR

George enters, carrying a thick wad of papers.

GEORGE: I've got it.

JENNY: George. (*She leans forward to kiss him*).

GEORGE: How are you feeling?

JENNY: Sleepy. All the better for your presence.

GEORGE: I've got the Mental Healthy Act. You know you can challenge their decision.

JENNY: Yes, the Nurse told me. Can you help me?

GEORGE: You'll need a lawyer. Do you know any?

JENNY: No.

GEORGE: You can represent yourself.

JENNY: So long as I don't swallow the medication. It makes me incapable of thought.

GEORGE: I'll help you prepare your appeal.

~ ENEMY TERRITORY ~

They lay out the papers on the bed and look at each section carefully. A huge gust of wind comes from the back stage and blows the papers around. George and Jenny chase them and catch them and end up laughing in each other's arms on the bed amid piles of crushed papers. Eventually they are all in one pile again.

GEORGE: It's this section.

Jenny and George are finally concentrating sitting on the bed.

GEORGE: Look, it's quite reasonable really, "No one can be detained without full written consent either from the client," see, they call you client, not patient … "themselves or according to severity of illness, a close relative or friend, or in the absence of the aforementioned, a social worker, or medical doctor or psychiatrist …" (*His voice falls.*) Just about anyone really …

JENNY: Why don't you tell them you're here? Then you can sign me out.

GEORGE: I'm not meant to be in this country. As far as they are concerned, I'm invisible. No, you must defend yourself, if I prepare it. I'll be back.

Exit George

SCENE FIVE

Twilight. The Nurse enters with a scanner on wheels and in the half darkness scans Jenny's womb. We see the foetus on a screen (either a large scanner screen or a projection above). It is moving, waving hands and jerking its bottom the way foetuses do. Suddenly the nurse stops and freezes the image. She calls a doctor on her beeper.

Enter Doctor, who examines the image.

NURSE: Hydraulic cortex.

DOCTOR: Spinal effusion. You're right. Freeze again.

In exasperation he takes the scanner from the Nurse and scans more.

Jenny wakes.

JENNY: I can see his hands. It's a boy isn't it? Is everything alright?

NURSE: The doctor has come because I detected an abnormality of the thorax, which means your baby will have difficulty breathing.

JENNY: But how can you possibly see – he's so small. Anyway he doesn't need to breathe.

NURSE:	Yet.
DOCTOR:	If you look carefully here (*enlarges the lung*), you will see white spots. These are pockets of fluid which have been preventing the lungs from growing for some time now. The baby is alright in the womb, but as soon as it is born, the lungs won't cope.
JENNY:	Don't be ridiculous. How can you tell anything from a picture a fuzzy as that?
DOCTOR:	There is a slim chance of survival. Sometimes the fluid dissipates, but that's rare.
JENNY:	(*Staring into space*) Now, do you see why I prefer to be mad?
DOCTOR:	No one said you were mad.
JENNY:	I prefer another world; this one is too mundane. It's too awful. And I know there's a better world, a world so beautiful, colourful and light that this one fades to nothingness. Why should I stay here where every step I take is blocked, where I am not myself. I can't say, "What a lovely day – I'll go for a walk." (*indicates window*) ... Bars. "What a lovely bump, at least I can hold sweet little

baby of my own." (*indicates scanner*) ... Lung problems. I can't get out of bed (*indicates glass*) medication. I can't think (*indicates glass*) medication. I can't even get a good cup of coffee – hospital food. What's the matter? Coffee's not difficult to make. (*Sits up*) Coffee's easy to make!

NURSE: This is bound to make you feel distanced.

JENNY: (*Furious*) Distanced! What does that mean? I'm here with this (*Indicates her bump*) and this (*the glass*). You're not, you're not bunged up in any way. You can't even imagine what it's like – feeling and yet not being allowed to, mothering and yet not being allowed to. Powerlessness is not and area of study, is it? It's not interesting to anyone. It's just (*breaks down*) crushing, crushing, crushing. Do you know ducks? You've seen them wild and alert and wagging their tails, well when their feathers get wet they have no strength, they get dirty and they can't get dry, they can't get the mud off and they can't keep warm. You know what happens? They die – they just die of cold and all because of their feathers. I can't even keep a duck in here.

Nurse and Doctor go to the edge of the stage and converse, ignoring the scene behind.

George enters carrying the duck.

JENNY: Oh, you've brought my duck, thank you.

George puts the duck on the bed. It settles down and allows itself to be stroked. It stays on stage till the end of the play.

GEORGE: I thought he'd keep you company.

Nurse and Doctor are in own spot, unheard by Jenny.

NURSE: She insists she sees her husband.

DOCTOR: She has a child's mind, children have imaginary friends. She has no husband, we know that. It's a form of schizophrenic wish-fulfilment; she creates her own husband, her own menagerie.

NURSE: How can she?

DOCTOR: We only use ten percent of our brains, the rest is a mystery, perhaps it's just full of hallucinations which come into play when the rest shuts down.

NURSE: So it has shut down.

DOCTOR: Well, pretty well … she wouldn't be here otherwise, would she?

NURSE: Dr Rolex assessed her and signed her in.

DOCTOR: Of course, he's perfectly competent. Given the circumstances, I would recommend termination. It's unlikely to reach full term anyway.

NURSE: It won't help her mental health.

DR COLEFAX: It is a medical complication.

NURSE: It would be kinder to induce her now, give her more time to recover. The post-natal hormonal drop will affect her anyway.

DOCTOR: Do you think she's in danger of hurting herself?

NURSE: No, she never talks about it.

JENNY: (*Waking*) Nurse.

NURSE: (*Going to her*) What is it?

JENNY:	I can't even talk to God anymore.
DOCTOR:	Well, what is it? Has she started?
NURSE:	Ah, no, she …
DOCTOR:	What?
NURSE:	She says she can't even talk to God anymore.
DOCTOR:	I'm sorry.
NURSE:	I don't know if you remember, but part of the original diagnosis was religious mania.
DOCTOR:	Then she's cured of one symptom at least. We just have to find a solution to the pregnancy and we are on our way to releasing a bed.
NURSE:	You realise that she is going to challenge the section in court tomorrow.
DOCTOR:	Y…Yes, yes, but it won't change anything. It's just an expensive formality, that's all.
NURSE:	I know it never happens, but if she did win, it would release a bed.

DOCTOR: Yes, I seeee. She's going to defend herself, I expect.

NURSE: That's right.

Exeunt Nurse and Doctor.

SCENE SIX

Night falls. George climbs in the window. Jenny wakes and is bright and responsive. George produces a sheaf of papers and they pore over them seated on the bed in the semi-darkness while the scene changes to that of a Courtroom.

As the lights come up, we see the Nurse and Doctor seated together on one side of a Courtroom, Jenny and the Duck on the other. It is a Mental Health Tribunal. There is no Jury, no Judge, but three Mental Health Adjudicators.

VOICE OFF: The court shall rise.

Enter the recognizable characters of Socrates, Roger Johnson and the Rabbi, dressed in pinstripe suits, who sit as the adjudicators.

DR COLEFAX: (*Rising*) We are here today for the appeal of Jenny Catchka against Section III of the Mental Healthy Act. I believe she is defending herself.

JENNY: I thought I'd do it myself, but I've left the papers in my room …

DOCTOR: Then, we must adjourn.

SOCRATES: I understood she was to have representation. I call on the counsel for Jenny Catchka.

Enter Kierkegaard in a pinstripe suit

SOCRATES: I call on Dr Colefax to put his case for the prosecution.

DR COLEFAX: Adjudicators, Jenny Catchka has been held under Section III of the Mental Healthy Act for a series of abnormal behavioural patterns that have lead to a diagnosis of manic depression. These are as follows: religious mania, hallucinations and uncontrollable weeping. At the moment her state of mind has no normal relationship with events in the world around her. For example if asked whether she wants cornflakes for breakfast she will talk about religious philosophy; if a male nurse enters the room, she bursts into tears. Sometimes she stays in catatonic states for up to 46 minutes. She talks to imaginary people who are clearly not present and appears to prefer the world of her imagination to real life. She has become incapable of dealing with the real world.

ROGER JOHNSON: Seems like a pretty watertight case …

RABBI: Please, we must hear the other side of the argument; the disputation!

KIERKEGAARD: (Rising) Ladies and gentlemen ... May I begin by questioning the first part of the diagnosis, that of religious mania. I have spoken with the appellant and her discussion of religion seems quite sound.

DR COLEFAX: It is not so much the substance of what she says as the frequency of the subject. God is an easy answer to everything: an escape from reality.

KIERKEGAARD: So she mentions God too much; how much is too much? May I point out that in every democratic society, freedom of religion is held paramount.

ROGER JOHNSON: Freedom of religion – oh yes, dodgy ground Dr Colefax.

SOCRATES: Indeed, a couple of millennia ago, discussion of the deities was considered a civic duty.

RABBI: Today the open discussion of the nature of God should be available to all – not regarded as an embarrassment.

DOCTOR: Adjudicators, can we argue on points of law, not personal opinion. All this talk of God is simply irrelevant.

SOCRATES: On the contrary Doctor, it is most interesting. Man strives constantly to be given some inspiration of God's law, he strives after all to be able as near as possible to imitate it. An open and frank discussion on its nature is the best means of approaching it.

RABBI: All your modern constitutions are based on the Law of Moses.

DR COLEFAX: May I bring the tribunal back to the case?

KIERKEGAARD: I will move on to the second part of the prognosis: that of hallucinations. Jenny has a highly developed imagination; this is a valuable gift, not a sign of madness. The fact that she spends hours thinking and imagining rather than sitting in front of a computer should not be considered outside of human norms. During her so-called catatonics she is simply in a state of heightened awareness which leaves her both more vulnerable and more mentally stimulated than day-to-day hospital life.

The fact that she prefers this world is to me quite understandable.

Thirdly, the evidence of uncontrollable weeping: surely this is a natural expression of grief for someone who has just lost her husband. Also her physical condition will make her nearer to tears than the average person. No, tears are not signs of madness, they are evidence of humanity! I would ask that the adjudicators decide to lift the section and allow Jenny her freedom.

DR COLEFAX : I think it is a mistake to seek to blame circumstances for Jenny's condition. It is insulting to assume that women spend their pregnancies weeping, many cope with demanding jobs. May I remind the adjudicators that mental illness is an illness like cancer or eczema – sometimes it is cured, sometimes not. We know it can be inherited. There are recognizable symptoms common to all cases, enough of which are displayed by Jenny Catchka. I would warn you that she is not yet capable of dealing with normal life, and that to release her would be a mistake.

The adjudicators mutter together for a few minutes, while the others sit tensely, apart from the duck, which is still wandering around.

Eventually the Rabbi rises.

RABBI: We three mental health adjudicators have decided, given the arguments put before us and having each concluded an interview with the appellant, that Jenny Catchka is to be released from Section III of the Mental Healthy Act and allowed to return to her life.

JENNY: (*Rising and beaming*) Thank you. Thank you very much.

SCENE SEVEN (HOSPITAL)

The scene turns around again and Jenny is standing by her bed packing a very small suitcase. She is wearing the clothes she wore at the beginning, but they are clean. She is no longer pregnant and has the duck on a lead.

Socrates and Kierkegaard in their clothes from Act One are at the foot of the bed in deep discussion.

KIERKEGAARD: You should very definitely not expect justice on this earth. If you want justice, you must die for it, for it exists only in the afterlife.

SOCRATES: Yes, and one of the perils of living an interesting life is that you often incur an interesting death.

JENNY: (*Holding out a palm-ful of pills*) You call these interesting?

SOCRATES: Come on, I drank hemlock. All you have to do is swallow six of them.

KIERKEGAARD: But you were forced to drink it, don't you remember? It's morally wrong, and if she takes these of her own accord, we can't be sure she'll join us. Pah! (*He slaps the bottom of Jenny's hand and the pills go flying.*)

SOCRATES: Look, I know how to get special dispensation … Just leave the gods to me …

JENNY: There's only one God …

The men walk off stage together as the light fades on the friendly scene.

Enter Claire, Jenny's sister, carrying the baby wrapped in a shawl.

CLAIRE: Come on, Jenny, the car's waiting. What are you doing hanging around here? Look, I've got him, what a perfect angel. You are so lucky …

THE END.

A PHANTOM LOVER
by Jean Findlay

Characters

ISOBEL .... a lady of 84
SALLY .... her cleaner, aged 24
JOSEPH .... Isobel's lover, aged 25

ACT ONE

A large front room in Marchmont, Edinburgh, with bay windows overlooking the Meadows. It is the beginning of the 21st century.

ISOBEL: I think he was attracted to me for my ideas, either my ideas or my nipples. Both were very prominent in those days.

She sits using her Zimmer.

Sally is dusting a carriage clock under a glass dome.

ISOBEL: Be careful with that. It has been broken before, by my last cleaner. She wasn't a real cleaner, just a poor girl.

Sally starts to dust the framed photo of a man.

SALLY: Well, I'm not a real cleaner either, I'm a student.

ISOBEL: Cookery, you call that a study! In my day you couldn't be a student without classical Arabic.

SALLY: (*Indicating photo*) Tell me more about him. Why was he attracted by your ideas?

ISOBEL: We both strongly believed in an independent Scotland.

SALLY: Good for you!

ISOBEL: That was radical then. Cookery students would've been unionists.

SALLY: Perhaps you could do your own cleaning in those days.

ISOBEL: I've never done my own cleaning. Ah ... Robbie was a fine man, a good thinker, a good lover, I wish I'd married him now ...

SALLY: I thought this was your husband.

ISOBEL: No, ... I wouldn't put him up. Just trying to shake his face out of my memory. There it was, day after day, leering across the breakfast table until I got him to take a daily paper. Then I could have my coffee in peace.

SALLY: Why didn't you divorce?

ISOBEL: Just for preference of another man? We weren't so trivial then. No, too much fuss. Not worth it. He wasn't a bad man, didn't hit me. Wasn't unfaithful. Loved me like a dog, a faithful labrador, always with his tongue hanging out.

SALLY: So they were both good men.

ISOBEL: Men aren't bad in general, just weak.

SALLY: Were you unhappy?

ISOBEL: Good heavens, no. There wasn't a day went past when I didn't thank God for my sleek hair, my good skin, my fine strong limbs, my generous husband, the fact that I lived off the fat of the land. For the first five years of marriage, life couldn't have been richer. I knew about the world, I wasn't cocooned, but I didn't experience its keener edges. I never knew hunger, I wore fine clothes, I mixed with the more interesting edge of society and I never experienced a stale bed.

SALLY: Did you feel there was something missing in your life, something spiritual perhaps?

ISOBEL: No, I did not. Bagwan Shree Rajneesh, at that point, had not made an appearance.

SALLY: *(Hurt. Shows the beads at her wrist).* These beads aren't from some funny Indian cult. This is a rosary.

ISOBEL: I beg your pardon.

SALLY: I'm a Marian Adventurer. We wear them tight so as not to forget.

ISOBEL: Forget what?

SALLY: *(Coming forward, new tone)* Let me tell you all about it.

ISOBEL: Oh no you don't, we're on six pounds an hour here. You haven't started that floor yet.

Sally exits and returns with a saintly, resigned face and a bucket and cloth. She gets down on her knees and starts to scrub.

ISOBEL: I do have a mop

SALLY: I prefer this position, it's the only way to clean a floor.

ISOBEL: As you please. You don't find it humiliating?

SALLY: Humbling, that's different.

ISOBEL: It wouldn't be something I'd seek out.

SALLY: *(Scrubbing)* They don't make floors like this anymore.

ISOBEL: No, they closed down the lino factory in Leith. It gave the workers emphysema – poison lung. The chemicals burnt little holes in the lung.

SALLY: *(Horrified)* Why don't you get rid of it?

ISOBEL: Like you say, they don't make it anymore.

SALLY: You could have laminated beech.

ISOBEL: It wouldn't have the same history.

SALLY: *(Stopping)* I hope you don't mind me asking, but I was wondering about your history.

ISOBEL: I'm 84.

SALLY: I'm not asking your age.

ISOBEL:	My most active and productive years were blighted by war.
SALLY:	Some people say it gave them a role.
ISOBEL:	I had a role all right. I was 23 when war broke out – that's what you say, isn't it? – "Broke out" – of course it didn't do so of its own accord …
SALLY:	No … people …
ISOBEL:	Yes, but this isn't a history lesson …
SALLY:	I wanted to ask about your role.
ISOBEL:	I was recruited by a large organization called the S.O.E.

Sally looks blank.

ISOBEL:	Special Operations Executive

Sally looks blank

ISOBEL:	It is now known as MI6.
SALLY:	Wow, you were a spy!

ISOBEL: We weren't called spies and it wasn't as wow as it sounds, it wasn't anything like a romantic war movie. It was all sadder, grimier and more pathetic than that.

SALLY: And you were forced into all sorts of immorality.

ISOBEL: That's the first time I've heard that one! You mean telling lies and killing people? Yes that's very immoral.

SALLY: The Fourth Commandment.

ISOBEL: Indeed. You're a fundamentalist?

SALLY: But what is even worse is the Sixth.

ISOBEL: The Sixth ... which is?

SALLY: Adultery.

ISOBEL: Aha.

SALLY: Apparently during the war because people always thought they'd die the next day, they gave no thought to sexual morality.

ISOBEL: Personally I would have thought killing more contentious, but I've done both.

SALLY: (*Horrified as with the lino.*) You poor soul.

ISOBEL: My dear girl, I employ you to clean, not to take pity on my soul.

SALLY: But I am concerned about your soul.

ISOBEL: Get out of my soul and back to your bucket.

Isobel picks up the telephone and dials.

"Martha ... Isobel ... of course ... am I ever ... You poor thing ... I pity you ... You don't like being pitied, neither do I ... But I mean it, flu's dreadful. You must stay in bed. Do you have any help? ... Elaine. She's alright but she takes advantage of your good nature. Get her to make chicken broth and have you any tonic wine? ... I'll send some over in a taxi right away. ... No, no, it's essential. Take some brandy with milk and honey as a night-cap ... Yes ... fine ... I've got Sally now. Great girl, she's here at the moment ... I read that ... Putin put it very well, "In Russia we know before the election who will become President. In America they can't even tell afterwards." ... What? ... Meant to be a Russian accent ... Thanks, I did live there, Martha. Yes I know it was all a long time ago ... No, Gore is too weak, he'll be swept away by all those right-wingers. There is a contemptible strain in American public life ... Roosevelt? You don't get many of them; a man of great moral and political integrity. ... Yes, I did. You know I did, Martha ... Oh, stop it ... I wouldn't be there now for anything. I'm quite happy in Edinburgh ... It's the most beautiful city in the world, and still on a human scale ... Alright, alright ... I'll shut up and you rest ...

All this while Sally is scrubbing the floor on her hands and knees. As Isobel comes off the phone, she rests.

SALLY: I'd like to work in telly.

ISOBEL: In the canteen?

SALLY: No, a lot of cooks go on telly.

ISOBEL: Good. Have you finished the floor?

SALLY: I wish you'd tell me about being a spy in the war.

ISOBEL: You know of the Official Secrets Act. I was not allowed to talk about it for fifty years. My experiences were not voiced or written

	down. I thought on them, yes, but if you can't give expression to them, memories become ... distant. For instance, how do you know about war, any war?
SALLY:	I do watch telly.
ISOBEL:	TV reports from some callow Oxbridge graduate staying at the local Hilton swapping stories, collecting impressions. Reports don't give an idea of the living experience. There's always no glamour, always more mud, more thieving, more cold.
SALLY:	Even in hot countries?
ISOBEL:	I was in Cairo in 1943. I boiled by day and froze by night.
SALLY:	Cairo in 1943, didn't you have good parties.
ISOBEL:	My God, yes. People were very different then; alive, young, intelligent. War stimulated the senses. People were more spirited, more generous, more alive to every human quality. Today I might go to a party and everyone will be beige like the carpet.
SALLY:	Tell me about Cairo.

ISOBEL:	Well, once we had a concert of songs we'd all written with lyrics that were more Rogers and Hart than Lloyd Webber. The real talent that was splattered across the sand! You've no idea. Then we danced as if there were no tomorrow – and for many of us there wasn't. Women were scarce, so I danced all the dances, and they were proper dances with steps and a necessary expertise, not just jiggling your body parts in front of a mirror which is what you do now. So little challenge for you in any area really. But as I was saying, there was a private, a proud, clever man, I don't think he stayed a private for long, anyway, he asked me to dance, which was unusual; only officers were allowed into the dance halls they had a stripe bar, rather like a colour bar – I don't know how he got in in the first place. He was Welsh and had a lovely voice – I told him so and asked him to keep on talking.
SALLY:	Did he?
ISOBEL:	No, he just looked at me with the sort of disdain the poor often have for the rich, the "You've never known life" look. Even you do it sometimes, although your poverty is temporary.

SALLY: You were being patronizing saying you liked his accent. It's like telling a black woman you like her hair.

ISOBEL: Nonsense. Both are compliments. He lacked the grace to accept a compliment. Perhaps it was just bad manners.

SALLY: It's more important to speak the truth. Manners are lies.

ISOBEL: I can see we're from different planets.

SALLY: Sorry, tell me about the Welsh private.

ISOBEL: Well ... Before I knew it, I was having an imaginary affair with him. An imaginary affair is always so much more satisfying than the real thing, don't you think?

SALLY: I've never had either. They are both wrong.

ISOBEL: Good God, lassie, what's wrong with you? Won't you ever live?

SALLY: I do live. I'm very happy with my life. It must be difficult getting old.

ISOBEL: (*Sharp*) Why do you say that?

SALLY: Today as I was leaving a shop, I stopped to let a very old couple go past. The woman had white hair and a pale face with careful makeup. Her bone structure was very good. She must have been a real beauty when she was young, but now, it was painful to take each step. The old man was helping her and the pavement was crowded. She looked at me as she passed …

ISOBEL: … as if she envied your youth.

SALLY: No, just because I let her pass.

ISOBEL: A twenty year old skin. (*Touches her*) There's nothing like it, taut, plump, shining. Perhaps she was just admiring you, we can also do that , you know, we old people. *(Rattles her zimmer)*.

SALLY: I'm sorry, I didn't mean to suggest –

ISOBEL: That I'm old. You don't need to, I am. You can even refer to it. You probably do: "I clean for an old lady", Mrs Old Lady, that's me.

SALLY: I can see you're hurt.

ISOBEL: Hurt, yes. But not by you dear. By life.

SALLY: You have to "deal with" hurt.

ISOBEL: Think how many hurts 84 years can pile on, especially war years. Think how many loved ones I've known killed.

SALLY: Lovers?

ISOBEL: I said loved ones. You have a one-track mind. Perhaps you ought to have it seen to – "deal with" it. (*Pause*) Yes, them as well. Lovers as well.

SALLY: The Welsh private …

ISOBEL: That's the power of erotic fantasy. Each day, at work in the office; endless paperwork and numbers in the dry heat; I'd create a different scene from our affair: a deliberate innuendo in conversation, leading to an electric touch of the fingers – a kiss, more kisses, embraces, passion, sex, sublime sex, truly sublime sex.

Sally is embarrassed.

ISOBEL: I can see you're embarrassed. That's good,

embarrassment is a healthy emotion. (*Pause*) It's important to have at least one fantasy lover. He can never make any mistakes, never stand on your foot, be indifferent to you, betray you; never fake an orgasm …

SALLY: Men can't.

ISOBEL: Shows how little you know. (*Pause*) He was called Joseph. Each time I saw him, we would look with such intensity, and all knowledge would pass between us in a matter of seconds. All knowledge of each other, I mean. I didn't need to take his clothes off: I knew what each part of his body felt like. I knew how smooth his skin was, how his shoulder blades moved, where his nose would fit as he kissed me, whether on my mouth or anywhere else. The more I thought about him, the more powerful he became, even when he was far off. He would burst in on my mind through the most serious work; talking to me gently, teasing, flirting …

SALLY: (*Interrupting, embarrassed*) But did he die? I just want to know if he died.

ISOBEL: No, a fantasy lover never dies. In fact he still visits me sometimes …

SALLY: You're sick ... that's really sick ...

ISOBEL: It's not sick. I can see him now. He has the most radiant face, he strides easily towards me. He is happy, young, strong. (*She gets up without her zimmer*) He will kiss me for hours ...

SALLY: Don't start that again.

ISOBEL: In those days, Sally, servants knew their place.

Isobel starts to walk easily across the stage. She is young again. The stage revolves as she walks round to reveal a verandah, palm trees, sand, blue sky. There are two wicker chairs facing each other on the verandah. On one of them sits Joseph, a very attractive young man, in khaki trousers, a white shirt and braces. He is smoking.

ISOBEL: I thought I'd find you here.

JOSEPH: Afternoon tea-parties, not my style. (*Rising*) Cigarette?

ISOBEL: Thanks. What is your style?

JOSEPH: (*Lighting it*). You are.

ISOBEL: (*Kissing him*) We can either kiss or smoke.

JOSEPH: For the benefit of the spectators, we'd better smoke.

They lean side by side on the verandah looking out, their bodies touching at the forearm. Pause.

ISOBEL: This is enough for me. I could stay here forever.

JOSEPH: No such thing as forever.

ISOBEL: There is, this is it.

JOSEPH: Desire, that's what this is. Just desire.

ISOBEL: What's "just" about desire. It's a whole world.

Joseph looks at her and bites her ear.

ISOBEL: Ow! (*Laughs*)

JOSEPH: Wake up, Izzy, I'll probably be under sand tomorrow.

ISOBEL: (*Suddenly sad and angry*) Don't say that, don't even think it.

JOSEPH: I want to go down the best of memories: your earlobes, neck , arms, breasts, legs, feet …

ISOBEL: You missed a bit out.

JOSEPH: (*Pressing himself against her*) But I won't, I won't miss it out, my love …

They snog in a romantic attitude while the stage revolves back to Sally finishing the scrubbing. She is hot and bothered.

SALLY: No, you shouldn't talk about things like that. A man who is going to his death, he should be thinking of his Maker, not profanities.

ISOBEL: (*Who has resumed her aged self*) Profanities? These are my body parts. You have them too. You have breasts.

SALLY: No.

ISOBEL: You do, you know, you may try to hide them, but they are there. What are they for?

SALLY: Feeding children, if I have any.

ISOBEL: You need to have sex first for that – and at the rate you are going …

SALLY: Stop talking about sex, I'm only here to clean your floor.

ISOBEL: And do the dusting and the kitchen, the bathroom, the bedroom … in fact you've a long way to go.

SALLY: I'd better get on with it.

ISOBEL: I've a new toilet cleaner. You leave it in the bowl for one hour, then scrub around the U-bend hard with the brush. Most people don't like to use the brush. I'm particular about the U-bend; I can't stand seeing stains and dark marks in it, it looks as though there's some faeces left behind.

SALLY: Alright I'll do the U-bend properly. Don't worry.

ISOBEL: And when you do the cloakroom, can you make sure you shine the taps. All a guest ever notices are the taps and if you shine them properly, he comes away with a clean, healthy feeling.

SALLY: Then they won't notice your U-bend.

ISOBEL: Aha. But I notice my U-bend, just as I notice the fingermarks on the mirror. Have you done this mirror Sally?

SALLY: Er ... no.

ISOBEL: Well, make sure you use window cleaner and a soft rag. Try not to leave any marks.

SALLY: Why do you have so many mirrors?

ISOBEL: "Vanitas, vanitatem, sayeth the preacher ..." You should know that one. I realise that all is indeed vanity so I may as well enjoy it if I can. (*Looking in mirror*). I enjoy this world. I don't think age is ugly: each line has a different story. You always retain your bone structure.

SALLY: I can't imagine aging.

ISOBEL: Luckily, it's gradual. Anyone with any sense accepts it.

SALLY: But it's sad just to think of you all alone with your mirrors, like Snow White's stepmother.

ISOBEL: (*Laughs, genuinely amused*) That's the funniest thing you've said. (*Pause*) I think it's really sad to imagine you all alone with your rosary beads.

SALLY: We have prayer groups.

ISOBEL: Perhaps I could set up a mirror group.

SALLY: You're the sad one; you don't live in the real world.

ISOBEL: My imaginary world is preferable to many real worlds. You, for example, know nothing of the nature of desire. It's not just because you are young and have fewer memories, it is also because you have very little imagination.

SALLY: (*In horrified tones*) I suppose you have a demon lover?

ISOBEL: "And all should cry – Beware! Beware!
His flashing eyes, his floating hair!
Weave a circle round him thrice
And close your eyes with holy dread,
For he on honey dew hath fed,
And drunk the milk of Paradise."

SALLY: I've heard that before, but I always thought the last part was about breast-feeding.

ISOBEL: (*Long, exasperated pause.*) No, it's a magic spell. I say it when I want my demon lover to appear.

SALLY: Oh, not that again. I wanted you to tell me about Cairo in the war.

ISOBEL: I'm trying to make it live for you. Listen: Multi-ethnic multi religious, these are modern words – we didn't use them then, but that's what Cairo was: Muslims, Copts, Jews, Christians, French, Italian, Greek all worked and played together. Then the war came and the British had to sort it all out, or thought they did – they interned half the French, all the Italians, except those employed by the Egyptians, all the Germans of course. Then the Australians and New Zealander's came. They were wilder than our lot. But they were given the fighting, not the thinking jobs.

SALLY: You had a thinking job.

ISOBEL: I spoke French like a native. I'd studied at the Sorbonne. There were a lot of us working on the French: the Vichy French, the French Resistance, the Egyptian bourgeois French. They weren't all on our side and you had to sort the sheep from the goats.

SALLY: What do you mean?

ISOBEL: During the day I worked in the code-office; that was my official job. There were dozens of decoders, all of us young women. In the evenings my job was socializing with the French – getting to know them as well as I could, listening to their gossip …

SALLY: So you were a real spy, like Mata Hari. Did you wear a sequined bra?

ISOBEL: Sequins were very difficult to obtain; so were bras for that matter. It wasn't glamourous, Sally. Exciting sometimes, but not glamourous. I was very tired. I worked all day in the office. Then everyone would go out to unwind and relax and I would go out too and would have to start acting – to pretend I was relaxing and having fun when I was doing very vital work, more important than the day job, and in another language.

SALLY: Didn't you enjoy it?

ISOBEL: A different personality would have loved it – a natural gossip with a natural zeal for the stuff of other people's lives; but then I would never have been chosen had I been a natural gossip. Discipline and discretion were the hallmarks of that occupation. Nor was I a natural show-off or actress; I disliked sequins.

SALLY: I don't like them either.

ISOBEL: But I did like silk. During the day I wore a roughly-made cotton khaki uniform, like every one else. In the evening I had to dress up, not like a British girl trying to impress the French; but like the French. That calls for a scientific bent.

SALLY: Where did you get the money for clothes like that?

ISOBEL: That was the real fun of the job. Good old special operations could get you anything. No one else could buy silk – all the worms in China were working for parachutes. But for me – la la la la la lallalalalal laa ... "Cinderella – you shall go to the ball!"
Of course I had to say I had a rich aunt – Aunt Special Operations.
Dressed by Aunt Special Operations, I would sally forth and chat up whoever I was told to chat up.

SALLY: Did you have to sleep with them to get the information?

ISOBEL: That was never ruled out. But in reality you get more out of someone through talking than through sex, especially if sex is at the back of their mind.

SALLY: Sex is never at the back of my mind.

ISOBEL: Are you sure?

SALLY: If ever I think of it I just start praying. It's the devil raising its ugly head, that's what sex is.

ISOBEL: You are a puritan.

SALLY: What's wrong with being a puritan? At least they are pure.

ISOBEL: Puritans are responsible for more evil in the world than decadents. Hitler was a puritan, so was Stalin. I've always seen Churchill as a decadent – at least compared to them.

SALLY: How can you say things like that?

ISOBEL: I've lived through these events, I've taken part in them, I've thought about them. When I was young we respected the thoughts of our elders.

SALLY: Well, I do, normally. I don't have to respect your fantasies, though.

ISOBEL: Don't you?
" … Beware! Beware!
His flashing eyes, his floating hair!
Weave a circle round him thrice
And close your eyes with holy dread,
For he on honey-dew hath fed,
And drunk the milk of Paradise."

SALLY: Stop it.

Joseph enters looking sand-blasted and confused. His clothes are torn and dirty and he is out of breath.

JOSEPH: Izzy, Izzy … Isobel.

He steps in the bucket and falls headlong across the stage.

JOSEPH: I'm under the sand. Isobel … Isobel … Izzy … No …

He loses consciousness.

The women go to him.

ISOBEL: Joseph! Joe …

SALLY: Who is he? What's he doing in here?

ISOBEL: Does that matter? Help him. I can't bend down. Sally. Help him.

SALLY: How?

ISOBEL: Brandy. In that cupboard.

Sally gets the brandy.

ISOBEL: Pour some in the lid. Give it to him.

Sally gets down on her knees and tries to administer the brandy.

ISOBEL: Lift his head with one hand … that's it. Use your head girl. Feed him.

After a while.

SALLY: I can't. He's not even breathing.

ISOBEL: Kiss of life.

SALLY: What?

ISOBEL:	Blow into his mouth.
SALLY:	How?
ISOBEL:	Put your lips over his. Hold his nose. Hand on the back of his head. (*Pause*) Do it … Please.

Sally does as Isobel directs. She puffs and waits, puffs and waits. She brings him back to life. His arms move up around her neck. They start to kiss. He pulls her down on top of him. Isobel stands back as they start to make love. This goes on for an uncomfortably long time before the curtain comes down.

End of Act One

ACT TWO

Cairo in 1943. The Gezira Club or Shepherds Hotel. An ornate table in the foreground with two chairs and some mint tea with glasses and behind, framing the whole, an ornate arch with white sunlight coming in, very bright. At the table are Isobel when young and Joseph.

JOSEPH: The desire for marriage is very bourgeois.

ISOBEL: I am bourgeois, I am deeply bourgeois. My family have been bourgeois for over ten generations.

JOSEPH: I can see you make no apologies.

ISOBEL: Apologies? For what I am?

JOSEPH: It's a state of mind – it's thoughtless, it's moribund ... it's not for me, Isobel.

ISOBEL: I thought we loved each other.

JOSEPH: I do, I love you body and soul; it's your mind that's the problem.

ISOBEL: You can't have civilization without the bourgeois, they govern, they educate, they medicate: they're the clergy, doctors, teachers.

JOSEPH: Besides, women should never propose.

ISOBEL: I always propose. Joseph, I have offered you my hand in marriage.

JOSEPH: A gallant gesture, I thank you for it but cannot accept.

ISOBEL: What do you want?

JOSEPH: Like most of the men here, I want complex conversation and uncomplicated sex.

ISOBEL: You won't get the second.

JOSEPH: Do you know how many brothels there are in Cairo?

ISOBEL: (*Rising scraping chair*) That's it.

JOSEPH: (*Holding her*) I'm joking. Sit down. I'm not about to go to a brothel.

(*Joseph lights up and chain smokes for the rest of the scene.*)

Enter Sally

SALLY: Did you call me?

ISOBEL: This is my maid, Sally. Sally, this is Lieutenant Evans.

Joseph shakes her hand.

ISOBEL: No, Sally, I'll stay a bit longer.

Exit Sally

JOSEPH: How did YOU get a maid? I thought everyone was meant to be doing vital work. I thought the reality of war put an end to all that rubbish.

ISOBEL: I AM doing vital work and I need support.

JOSEPH: I suppose you need someone to dress you.

ISOBEL: I don't talk about my work.

JOSEPH: I could dress you. Would you pay me?

ISOBEL: Enough sarcasm.

JOSEPH: I'm being sincere.

ISOBEL: As far as you are concerned, she could be my Arabic interpreter.

JOSEPH: Cunningly disguised as a maid, when no one else but the Queen of Egypt has maids. It's a really good disguise.

ISOBEL: I can see the conversation is going nowhere. Sally!

Enter Sally, speaking Arabic.

ISOBEL: Were you listening?

SALLY: No.

ISOBEL: Why not? I've told you to listen, always.

SALLY: Asked, not told.

JOSEPH: Quite right, ASKED, Isobel, ASKED.

ISOBEL: She's meant to be my maid.

JOSEPH: It won't wash. It's hopeless. Who gave you that idea?

ISOBEL: The C in C.

JOSEPH: *(Laughing)* It won't wash, Izzy.

ISOBEL: Don't patronise me, Joseph.

JOSEPH: The C in C said a maid was a good idea, for who?

ISOBEL: Perhaps you are a member of the communist party, Joe, but those in power here, the Egyptians, the British and the French still have domestic servants.

JOSEPH: With fluent Arabic? A girl like that from Britain. You've got to move with the times, Isobel. She should be cracking codes …

ISOBEL: She IS cracking codes.

JOSEPH: For who?

ISOBEL: I can't tell you.

JOSEPH: Alright but it's a bad disguise, a bad example. In two years time you'll see

	communist governments in three of the Allied countries – you wait.
ISOBEL:	Where?
JOSEPH:	Yugoslavia, Greece, France.
ISOBEL:	France? You are crazy. Communism won't sit in a sophisticated civilization.
JOSEPH:	Alright, socialism, enlightened socialism. It'll happen in Scotland too. Do you want to bet on it?
ISOBEL:	Bet? Gambling's the first thing an enlightened socialism would stop.
JOSEPH:	Then it wouldn't be very enlightened. *Long pause.* Falling out of love is as unstoppable as falling in love.
ISOBEL:	And we are mere toys for the gods to play with. Rubbish, you can't build a society like that.
JOSEPH:	Who's building a society?
ISOBEL:	We all are. We all will be after this. I thought

	you agreed on at least that score. You've got to have a desire for the warmth, the depth of family feeling.
JOSEPH:	Yuk. Stodge.
ISOBEL:	No, it's very attractive.
JOSEPH:	Like suet pudding is attractive?
ISOBEL:	It is.
JOSEPH:	On that note, I shall return to the barrack and hope we have suet pudding.
ISOBEL:	No, stay. *Pause.* Where is she?
ISOBEL:	Who?
JOSEPH:	Sally, the lovely maid.
ISOBEL:	She is hard-working, efficient, but lovely?
JOSEPH:	I think she is.
ISOBEL:	(*Calling*) Sally, get the bill.

Sally gets the bill and holds it.

ISOBEL	Give it to Joe.
JOSEPH:	You expect me to pay?
ISOBEL:	Of course, you're a man.
JOESEPH:	You are better paid.
ISOBEL:	I expect men to pay in restaurants, it's part of European civilization.
JOSEPH:	We're not in Europe.
ISOBEL:	I don't care, it's only tea. I didn't have any opium.
JOSEPH:	It's just as cheap … just teasing. Of course I'll pay.

He brushes her forehead with his lips.

Sally spits.

ISOBEL:	Sally!
SALLY:	Yes.
ISOBEL:	You spat!

SALLY: Sorry I got a fly in my mouth.

ISOBEL: Don't you know the polite way to remove something from your mouth? Watch.

(Isobel takes a sugar lump, puts it in her mouth, coughs into her closed hand, opens her palm like a magician to reveal the sugar lump on her hand).

SALLY: If I did that with the fly ...

ISOBEL: Yes?

SALLY: (*Mimes it*) Ridiculous.

Joseph mimes the fly flying off her hand all around the room, eventually landing on Isobel where he swats it.

JOSEPH: Sorry.
(*To Sally*) Have a sugar lump, takes away the taste of fly.

Sally takes it flirtatiously from his palm and eats it.

ISOBEL: Joseph!

JOSEPH: I didn't cough on it.

Sally and Joseph giggle.

ISOBEL: This is too much. It's the heat. Anyway I don't need opium, I've got a mind. I've got to finish a translation.

JOSEPH: From what to what?

ISOBEL: Don't ask.

JOSEPH: Don't worry, I'll guess. Ancient Hebrew to Greek, Greek to Arabic, Arabic to French and French to code. Then it'll be cracked by another SOE operative and they'll translate it back all the way, file it, lock it up, label it top secret, guard it and leave it til after the war's over. That's what happens to most of your stuff isn't it? It's very useful.

ISOBEL: My work IS useful and yours is too.

JOSEPH: I'll go out into the hot desert in a hot tin box and be boiled alive, exploded all over the sand.

ISOBEL: Don't ... calm down, have some more tea. (*Pours tea.*)

JOSEPH: Pass the sugar.

ISOBEL:	I have to do these translations, you have to do those exercises.
JOSEPH:	Pass the sugar, could you?
ISOBEL:	They say the first translation is the most important; I know it is.
JOSEPH:	Do you think I could have the …

Sally, who has been listening and watching from behind, takes the sugar and passes it to Joseph who looks at her – grateful and flirtatious

JOSEPH:	(*Triumphant*) You do listen. She does listen Izzy.
SALLY:	One or two.
JOSEPH:	Three.
ISOBEL:	Three sugars?
JOSEPH:	I've got to keep awake.
ISOBEL:	Why?
JOSEPH:	I'm going out there tonight. You know that. You're doing a very important translation and don't have time for anything more civilized.

ISOBEL: Like what?

Joseph gets up takes her in his arms and waltzes round the stage. Music. More wildly, more passionately. Starts to kiss her and she breaks away.

ISOBEL: Civilized? (*Sits*)

JOSEPH: Yes.

Sally steps forward, eyes locked and waltzes with him round and round and round to music and out of the room.

Isobel is left alone, clutching her large handbag. She pours more tea. Puts down her bag. Slowly takes one, two, three, four sugars. Takes out her translation and gets on with it.

Passage of time.

Sally and Joseph enter holding hands, laughing, a little drunk.

ISOBEL: (*Looking at watch.*) Where have you been?

SALLY: At a club, Groppi's.

ISOBEL: You're meant to be my maid. You can't go to Groppi's

SALLY: No one recognized me, did they, Joe?

JOSEPH:	Everyone's too drunk by this time – we didn't stay long.
SALLY:	We went for a walk.
JOSEPH:	Under the frangipani blossom.
SALLY:	And the orange trees – the wonderful scents.
JOSEPH:	Blossom, wood smoke, sweat, spices, intoxicating.
ISOBEL:	Joseph ? (*Broken*)
JOSEPH:	Yes?
ISOBEL:	Nothing. I've finished the translation. Yes, Cairo is wonderful. The smells … We are not obliged, you and I, in any way, are we? You did kiss me though, didn't you?
JOSEPH:	Did I? Did I really? Did you imagine it? I did kiss Sally tonight.
SALLY:	He did.

End of Act Two

ACT THREE

Back in Marchmont, Edinburgh 2001. Isobel is 84. She rattles her Zimmer, waiting.

ISOBEL: Where is she …? Sally, the lovely maid … ha!

Sally enters with her own key.

SALLY: I'm sorry I'm late.

ISOBEL: Why are you late? I was waiting … It's confusing when someone is late.

SALLY: I was meeting someone.

ISOBEL: A man?

SALLY: Yes, a boyfriend.

ISOBEL:	Good. You were making love.
SALLY:	No, talking, just talking.
ISOBEL:	I'm glad.
SALLY:	Even though I'm late.
ISOBEL:	How?
SALLY:	How what?
ISOBEL:	How did you get a boyfriend?
SALLY:	I just did, you inspired me. Your story about Cairo, your war work.
ISOBEL:	My work was insignificant. I didn't tell you much.
SALLY:	No, but about your life, the life you led.
ISOBEL:	About the city and Joseph?
SALLY:	Yes
ISOBEL:	Huh, I didn't say much.
SALLY:	You did. You have a great way of telling

	things. I've never heard anything so vivid. I could smell it.
ISOBEL:	That smell; spices and manure, sweat, wood smoke, mint, alcohol.
SALLY:	Your parties, better than telly.
ISOBEL:	The one with the king, King Farouk. Someone gave me a couple of turkeys. We had Nile fish and prawns and strawberries and cream and Palestinian wine cup. There were six nice, attractive men in Cairo and they were all there. The festivities were wonderful, absolutely spontaneous with dervishes and sword swallowers dancing among gay crowds, and native orchestras, and barrows selling melons and honey cakes, rice and beans, coloured wines and flags …
SALLY:	What happened?
ISOBEL:	You know. Rommel was defeated. Joe died.
SALLY:	He DID die.
ISOBEL:	He was blown up in a tank. Boiled and exploded, scattered across the sand.

SALLY: You loved him.

ISOBEL: Him and others.

SALLY: Him above all.

Isobel starts to cry. Sally comes forward and holds her.

SALLY: I'm sorry. I'm so sorry.

THE END

LITTLE BLACK RAINCLOUD

a play in one act

by Jean Findlay

Characters

JESS .... a new mother in her thirties with her four-month-old baby, Luther
JOHN .... her husband
CATHY .... a neighbour and friend
CALUM .... Jess's brother
RADIO VOICES – pre-recorded

A kitchen living-room in West London. There are lots of books, piles of periodicals, and framed photojournalism on the walls. A happy mother is breast-feeding a four-month-old baby at the kitchen table before brown bread, organic marmalade and a coffee pot.

Enter John, who is thin and intense.

JOHN: Yes, good morning. Did you sleep well?

JESS: Not much. Luther had a hungry night.

JOHN: You've eaten a whole loaf!

JESS: It's hard being a cow.
Have some coffee.

JOHN: Is there any hot milk?

JESS: In the pan.

John turns on the radio.

RADIO: "A British Officer was killed yesterday in Iraq. A group from the Little Prince's Regiment were eating their lunch under a tree when a suicide bomber jumped out of the tree on top of them.

John turns it off

JOHN: I've had enough of this unnecessary war, concocted by phoney philosophers, right-wingers, anti-semites. I knew all along people would get killed.

Jess stands with baby on breast and pours milk from the pan into John's coffee.

JESS: People usually do in war.

John turns it on again.

RADIO: "Chris Wilcox, spokesman for the PPR Tank advises that the next protocol for gas emissions from the Saganaki Argeement should be reconsidered in the light of ..."

John turns off the Radio,

JOHN: Chris Wilcox. I knew it. I was at College with him. Think tanks are a relief mechanism for the otherwise unemployable middle-classes. A meeting of mediocre minds.

Luther cries. Jess gets the changing mat and puts it on table.

JOHN: Not on the table, it's unhygienic.

Jess puts it on the floor and kneels to change him. She hums.

JOHN:	I think it's going to rain.
JESS:	(*Sings from Disney's "Winnie the Pooh"*) "I'm just a little black rain cloud Hovering under the honey tree. I'm just a little black rain cloud Pay no attention to me. Everyone knows that a rain cloud Never eats honey, no not a bit …"
JOHN:	(*Looking out of window*) It may rain. I wonder if I should take the gamble and go for a walk.

John puts hand in pocket and carefully counts £5 in £1 coins handing it to Jess.

JOHN:	That's for today.
JESS:	I need to buy nappies.
JOHN:	How much?
JESS:	Seven pounds thirty five.
JOHN:	How long will they last?
JESS:	Depends how often Luther poos.

JOHN: How many in a packet?

JESS: Thirty-two. He can manage on three a day … that's ten days.

JOHN: Eleven days.

John counts out the money.

JOHN: I'm going for a walk.

JESS: I was going to take Luther out in the pram.

JOHN: That will do you both good. Have a nice walk.

JESS: See you later.

Exit John

Jess dresses Luther in his outdoor clothes, humming. She puts him in the pram. The axle breaks. She takes the baby out, puts him on the floor, gets tape from a drawer and fixes the axle. She puts the baby back in, fetches a hat for him and finds her own coat.

The doorbell rings.

Jess opens the door. It is Cathy, her neighbour, carrying a bag of apples.

CATHY: Windfalls. (*Kisses her*) Are you going out?

JESS:	I was. But look, he's asleep now anyway. (*Takes off her coat*)
CATHY:	We should peel these now or they'll bruise.
JESS:	Day off?
CATHY:	Two days off. I'd rather deal with bruised apples than bruised humans …

She tips them on the table as Jess takes her coat. They sit at the table. Jess gets out knives.

JESS:	(*Sighing*) Look at that. There's nothing like it. A sleeping baby. Perfect peace.
CATHY:	Or a dead body.
JESS:	(*Alarmed*) What do you mean?
CATHY:	Just that stillness. Peace. You could stare at him forever and not do anything else, not peel apples …
JESS:	Or talk to our husbands.
CATHY:	Where is he, that cranky old husband of yours?

JESS:	He's not old, he's young. He's gone for a walk.
CATHY:	Could've taken the baby.
JESS:	He would never take him.
CATHY:	Perhaps when he's grown up a bit.
JESS:	Maybe when he's six.
CATHY:	(*Laughs*) I meant John. Never mind. (*Pause*) Why on earth did you call him Luther?
JESS:	It was John's idea. He did his dissertation on the Reformation. At least it's unusual. There won't be any others in the nursery.
CATHY:	Nooooooooooooooo.
JESS:	Or the playground.
CATHY:	He can always change it later on.
JESS:	People don't.
CATHY:	Your brother did.

JESS:	Calum?
CATHY:	Lorry. He used to be called Lorry.
JESS:	No. Calum is his real name. Lorry was just a nickname. It was his first word as a baby. Better than tractor.
CATHY:	Or tank. How is he, your Lorry?
JESS:	Just lost his job.
CATHY:	I thought he was in the army.
JESS:	Yes, his whole regiment was cut.
CATHY:	That's awful.
JESS:	John says it's better to lose your job than your life.
CATHY:	Don't quote John. I hate it when you quote John. What does he know? Has he got a job yet?
JESS:	Yes, he has.
CATHY:	What?

JESS:	Two days a week in a Government think tank.
CATHY:	Think tank? Like a fish tank?
JESS:	Lots of thinkers discussing things round a table.
CATHY:	And he gets paid for that? Does he have to wear a tie?
JESS:	Pay yes. Tie no. He's very happy. How's your love life?
CATHY:	I hate it when people ask that. What they mean is how's your sex life? Do I have sex in the laundry cupboard with a dashing doctor – dashing in and dashing out? That only happens in soaps.
JESS:	I don't mean that.
CATHY:	The answer is zero. I've been in Intensive Care for the last six weeks and I can't imagine anything worse than a man making eyes at me as I pull the tubes out of someone for the last time. Anyway most of the doctors are women. They think I'm a doctor just because I speak English and know what the tubes are called.

JESS: Tubes?

CATHY: Drip feed, Heart monitor, Catheter – Marble Arch, Bond Street, Oxford Circus.

Jess laughs. Both laugh.

Enter John

Both stop laughing.

CATHY: (*Rising, going to greet him*) Hello, John.

JOHN: (Avoiding her) Hello. (*to Jess*) I'm afraid I got caught in the rain.

JESS: Oh, I'm sorry.

JOHN: I knew it was going to rain.

John takes off his coat and drops it on the floor. Jess goes to pick it up.

JOHN: Well, nice to see you, Cathy. I'm sure you'll drop round again soon.

JESS: We're just peeling some apples. Cathy brought them.

JOHN:	That's very kind of you. Thank you. Well. Goodbye.
CATHY:	(*Good naturedly*) You're a welcoming old soul. I'll get my coat. Bye Jess.
JOHN:	I'll see you out. (*Holds door for her*)

Exit Cathy

JESS:	John.
JOHN:	She's always here, coming in for a gossip. You'd think she had nothing else to do. You'll see her again. I think I've caught a fever.

John collapses on the sofa.

Luther stirs. Jess picks baby up.

JESS:	Shall I get you a warm drink?
JOHN:	Thank you.
JESS:	Camomile tea?
JOHN:	Please.

Jess puts on the kettle and clears up the apple peelings while holding Luther.

JOHN: I think I may have pneumonia.

JESS: Why don't you go to bed? You need to take off your wet clothes.

JOHN: Will you take them off?

Jess tries to take off his shoes while holding the baby.

JESS: No, John. You do it. Take off your clothes and go to bed.

John gets up painfully from the sofa and exits. Jess heaves a sigh of relief and sinks onto the sofa with Luther. She hums.

Passage of time.

The doorbell rings. Jess opens the door.

Enter Calum, her brother, in his kilt, carrying a large package wrapped in coloured paper. He puts down the package and picks up Jess and the baby swinging them round.

JESS: Calum!

CALUM: Hey. Hellooo. Come to see my new nephew.

	(*Takes baby from her and holds him*) What a handsome wee lad! Good strong legs. I've brought you a present. Wait till you see what your uncle Calum has for you. Is he eating yet?
JESS:	Why, what's that? A haunch of venison?
CALUM:	What a lovely bairn you have, Jess. But how are you?
JESS:	Hungry most of the time, like Luther.
CALUM:	Luther?
JESS:	That's his name.
CALUM:	Why?
JESS:	It was John's idea. It's unusual.
CALUM:	It is ... But there's probably a reason for that. Where is John?
JESS:	In bed with a chill. He got caught in the rain today.
CALUM:	They're wicked these raindrops.

JESS: John is a brilliant man with a delicate constitution.

CALUM: What's he doing these days with his brilliance?

JESS: He's got a job in a Government think tank.

CALUM: Well, good for him. I've lost mine.

JESS: Mum said you lost your job.

CALUM: Don't get me started. It wasn't my job it was my life. I'm not taking off my kilt until I get another.

JESS: (*Pause*) It'll get dirty.

CALUM: I won't sleep in it. Jess, don't you understand? That was my whole life. We worked hard, we played hard, we lived hard. I haven't been bored in ten years. I owe my regimental tartan something. I'm not taking it off until I find a job.

JESS: (*Hesitantly*) I suppose there's some reason in that.

CALUM: There doesn't have to be. You've no idea what I've lost.

JESS: Oh, Calum. I'm so sorry. I lost my job when I had Luther.

CALUM: Ok. (*Smiles*) But he's great compensation.

JESS: You'll find another.

CALUM: Can I stay here?

JESS: Of course. There's a spare room. (*Pause*) You don't have a bag.

CALUM: I travel light.

JESS: We should open the present.

CALUM: Wait till he wakes. (*Baby has gone to sleep in his arms*)

Enter John

Calum rises to greet him. John stiffens.

CALUM: John.

JOHN: Calum.

They shake hands.

JOHN: It's been a long time.

CALUM: Not since that memorable day at Marylebone Registry Office, with you in your best jeans.

JOHN: You were wearing your kilt then, I recall.

CALUM: Haven't taken it off since.

JOHN: Joke, I hope.

CALUM: It's comfy. It's got style.

JOHN: You won't catch Luther wearing a kilt. (*Sees large present*) What's that?

CALUM: Present for my nephew.

JOHN: What is it?

CALUM: Surprise.

JOHN: Can't we open it?

CALUM: Wait till he's awake. He's sleeping so peacefully.

JESS: Can you put him in his cot, Calum? First left at the top of the stairs.

Exit Calum

JESS: (*calling after him*) ... and yours is the room opposite.

JOHN: He's not staying is he?

JESS: He's come to London to find a job. His whole regiment was cut.

JOHN: I know that.

JESS: I said he could have the spare room.

JOHN: But that's my study.

JESS: You can move your computer to the bedroom. I don't mind.

JOHN: But I do. He can't stay here.

JESS: He is. He's my brother.

JOHN:	Does he drink?
JESS:	I'm sure he does.
JOHN:	We can't have an alcoholic in the house. We have a small child.
JESS:	There's no evidence to suggest he's an alcoholic.
JOHN:	He's bound to be a right-winger.
JESS:	There's no evidence for that either.
JOHN:	He's been in the army for ten years. He must believe in the use of force. That's right-wing. Perhaps he can get a job as a bouncer in a night-club.
JESS:	Don't be stupid. He's an officer.
JOHN:	Was. Or the police perhaps. And why is he wearing a kilt? He's obviously cracked.
JESS:	I thought you were tolerant of other cultures.
JOHN:	Most ex-soldiers end up on the streets drinking meths.

JESS: Thanks. That's helpful.

JOHN: You can't give him a key. It's a security risk.

JESS: Soldier, Bouncer, Policeman. My brother is not a security risk.

Enter Calum

JESS: Did you find your room?

CALUM: I'd prefer a sea view.

JESS: Sorry, we only do brick walls.

JOHN: That's my study, which has a bed in it.

CALUM: I can see that. I don't want to put you to any bother.

JESS: John, here's your tea. You ought to go to bed with that chill.

Exit John. Jess and Calum sit down. Pause.

CALUM: You sound like a Victorian nanny. Where's my old Jessie?

JESS: He can be difficult when he's ill.

CALUM: Look I'll kip down here. I won't use his study. (*Listens*) He's gone up there now anyway. I can't use it.

JESS: You didn't bring a bag.

CALUM: I just brought The Present.

JESS: Oh, yes. We must open it.

CALUM: Not till he wakes.

Jess goes to a drawer and brings out a new toothbrush in a packet.

CALUM: Oh. Thank you.

JESS: Underpants?

CALUM: No.

Jess exits and returns with a duvet, pillows and sheets. She makes the sofa up as a bed.

Jess kisses her brother on the head.

JESS: Night … night.

CALUM: God, I'm tired.

Exit Jess.

Calum takes off kilt. He is wearing a long white shirt. He gets under the duvet.

Passage of time. Night.

Calum is on the sofa, sleeping.

Suddenly, the light is switched on by John. Calum jumps out of bed and is standing upright, urine running down his leg.

CALUM: Shit!

JOHN: That too?

CALUM: No … What are you here for?

JOHN: Would you like some camomile tea?

CALUM: No! *(Furious)* I wouldn't. I have this.

(slams whisky bottle on table)

JOHN: That's why you wet the bed.

CALUM: No again! It's not! *(Angry)* You don't get it do you?

(Sits at table. Swigs)

JOHN: That's my sofa.

Calum takes him by the collar and lifts him up.

CALUM: Shut up, wanker.

(*Sits him on chair*) Now shut it. What do you know? Think tank. Which department?

JOHN: Exchequer.

CALUM: Department of cuts.

JOHN: Exchequer is above Defense.

CALUM: That makes a lot of bloody sense, doesn't it? Especially when you're at war. (*Pause*) You lot came up with the idea to cut the army. YOU. What do you know?

JOHN: Wait a minute. It wasn't me personally. I contributed. The rationale behind it is …

CALUM: (*Shouts*) Rationale. (*takes sgian dubh knife out of his sock*)

JOHN: Let me call the police.

CALUM: Wait a minute, wee scaredy cat. I'm not going to hurt you. Have you ever seen a weapon before?

JOHN: No, I'm against violence.

CALUM: You would be. So are we all, believe it or not, but some of us have to do a job called peace-keeping. (*Pause*)
Cuts, bloody cuts.

(Pause, then he takes the knife and cuts the inside of his own arm three times until the blood runs down.)

JOHN: Aaaaagh. You're mad.

CALUM: You've probably never even seen blood before.

JOHN: I don't like the sight of blood.

CALUM: Did you not see your own son being born?

JOHN: I can't bear the sight of blood.

CALUM: Well, what you normally do is (*gets up and takes the kitchen roll and winds it round his arm*) ... help to stop it.

JOHN: I think you need a doctor.

CALUM: I need more than a doctor. (*Swigs whisky*) I watched my best friend die. I watched him bleed to death beside the road, waiting for help. I asked him to hang on. I begged him to hang on. He just drained away before my eyes.

(Drains bottle)

Now he'd have lost his job too. Some thanks.

JOHN: Better to lose your job than your life

CALUM: (Mimicking in namby pamby way) "Better to lose your job than your life." He lost both!

JOHN: But you haven't.

CALUM: Are you trying to say you saved my life?

JOHN: I don't believe in the use of violence. Less soldiers, more peace.

CALUM: Less soldiers, more peace. More peace, better economy. Is that how it works? Let's see, better economy, more weapons. More weapons, more violence. More violence …

	oooops, where's all the soldiers? We moved them off the board ages ago. Where are they all? On social security, drinking meths, in the Salvation Army hostels wearing your old t-shirts, the ones with Che Guevara on them. Good ol' Che, he'd never allow himself to be castrated like this. Let's hear it for a bit of South American manhood. We Europeans haven't had that impulse since the Middle Ages. But no, there's nothing useful for you to do. Sorry, mate. We can give you handouts and a therapist so you can complain about your bad back on a weekly basis …
JOHN:	(*Coldly*) Why don't you become a policeman? Then you can catch robbers.

Enter Jess

JESS:	Hey! Calum … John, did you …?
JOHN:	No, I didn't.
CALUM:	I did it myself.
JOHN:	He needs a doctor. You should go up to A and E.
CALUM:	No way. It's just a wee cut.

JESS:	(*Picking up phone*) Hello. Cath? Sorry to wake you. Lorry's here and he's cut himself – quite badly. Can you come with a bandage or something? … Come now. (*phone down*) Cathy's coming.
JOHN:	You shouldn't have bothered her. It's unfair in the night. He can go to A and E.
CALUM:	Is that Cathy? Your old friend Cathy?
JESS:	Yes. She lives in London now. Moved into this street. You remember her?
CALUM:	You bet. She's worth a slashed arm!

Calum gets up, puts on his kilt. Sees that his shirt is all bloody. Takes it off. Sits at the table in kilt and kitchen roll.

JOHN:	Listen to him, he's drunk.
JESS:	Calm down, you two.

The doorbell rings.

Jess opens the door to Cathy with her First Aid box. She stops and stares at Calum who looks devastating in kilt and kitchen roll, then collects herself.

CATHY: Hello, Lorry. Did you have a crash?

Calum gets up and goes to greet her.

CALUM: You haven't changed a bit.

CATHY: Sit down. How did you do that?

CALUM: It's not serious. I did it to make a point.

JOHN: It's called self-cutting: a neurotic trait mainly found in women.

JESS: Will you go, John?

Calum starts unrolling the kitchen roll on his arm.

CATHY: I thought you were in Iraq.

CALUM: I lost my job.

CATHY: It'll need a tight bandage.

JOHN: Some job, killing people. Much safer self-cutting in London.

CATHY: Can I have some water, Jess?

Jess hands a bowl to Cathy and a cup to John.

JESS: Go to bed, John.

CATHY: Tell me if it hurts.

CALUM: (*Wincing*) Doesn't hurt at all.

JOHN: Goodnight. I can't bear all this macho posturing.

Exit John

Cathy bathes the cut and bandages it.

JESS: I'm going to bed too. If you don't mind, Cath.

CATHY: No, no. I've handled worse.

Exit Jess

Cathy pins the bandage.

CALUM: Yeow!

CATHY: Serves you right. You'd be recommended for therapy if you'd taken this to a doctor.

CALUM: (*Admires bandage*) That's a fine job. I'd offer you a drink, but I've finished the whiskey.

CATHY: I can smell that.
(Opening fridge) There's half a bottle of wine here.

CATHY: Are you trying to get me drunk?

Cathy pours herself a glass, but not Calum.

CALUM: I see, no more for me. You really haven't changed.

CATHY: Nor have you. You did that to make a point. I must at least have gained some maturity in the last ten years.

CALUM: Wisdom. It looks like wisdom. What about me?

CATHY: (*Studies him*) Not so much wisdom … more experience. (*studies bottle*) "Isle of Raasay" single malt. You have exotic tastes.

CALUM: Only in women.

CATHY: I'm not exotic. I'm very straightforward. But you like variety.

(Calum looks ashamed)

CATHY:	Shame is a redeeming quality.
CALUM:	Does that mean you forgive me?
CATHY:	(*Pause*) Of course. It was a long time ago. I'm sure you've learnt better.
CALUM:	You're so optimistic.
CATHY:	Hopeful. Hope is like bubbles. It always rises so long as there's life.
CALUM:	(*Pause*) I have also learnt not to seize obvious innuendos.
CATHY:	Good.
CALUM:	I was meaning to get in touch. I wanted to say … sorry, I suppose I wish we could pick up where we left off, as if nothing had happened in ten years.
CATHY:	What about all my wisdom?
CALUM:	And all my whisky?
CATHY:	I'm sure you're an expert.
CALUM:	I could set up a consultancy. Calum Bain:

Malt Whiskey Consultant. (*Brightens*) Actually, that's a good idea. London's the only place for it.

Pause.

CATHY: What are you thinking?

CALUM: (*With natural grace*) Whether 'tis nobler in the mind to sit still and suffer the slings and arrows of desire, or to lean across the table and kiss you.

CATHY: (*Laughs*) You can kiss me.

Calum kisses her lightly on the lips across the table.

CALUM: (*Brightly*) That was nice. Can I do it again?

CATHY: (*Laughs*) Go on …

Calum does so.

CALUM: And again.

They are both laughing more and more. They stand and embrace.

Enter John.

They separate.

JOHN: What's going on? There's a child upstairs.

CATHY: Yes, but he's not watching.

JOHN: First you wet my sofa, now you're having sex on it.

CATHY: We're not!

JOHN: You're practically naked.

Calum lifts his kilt in John's direction, with back to audience.

CATHY: Oh, yes, so I am.

Calum stifles a laugh.

JOHN: Slut! On my sofa!

CALUM: (*Instant anger*) What did you say? Pervert, voyeur, misogynist. If you weren't married to my sister …

CATHY: Boys, break it up.

Enter Jess in a nightie with howling baby Luther. They are all silent and listen to the howling.

JESS: He's done a poo. Did I leave the nappies here?

Cathy gets nappies. Jess lays a changing mat on the table.

JOHN: (*Angry*) Not on the table, it's unhygienic.

JESS: He's on a mat. Anyway, it's only baby poo – your own baby's poo. It won't kill you.

CATHY: I've just done first aid here. Calum's blood is far more lethal. All you do, John, is scrub the table.

JESS: John's never scrubbed a table.

JOHN: You think ...

Jess starts singing to quieten Luther as she changes him.

> "I'm just a little black rain cloud
> Hovering under the honey tree.
> I'm just a little black rain cloud.
> Pay no attention to me.
> Everyone knows that a raincloud never eats honey ..."

She has a lovely voice and Calum and Cath sit and listen. It calms the baby and calms them.

There is a loud rumble.

Long pause.

JOHN: Thunder.

CALUM: (*Putting on his shirt and tucking it in.*) It's not thunder.

Silence. Another rumble.

CALUM: Turn on the radio.

RADIO: Breaking news of a severe explosion in Paddington Station. Residents West of that area are advised to Go in, Stay in and Tune in. *Musak.* Please refer to your Government leaflet, "Go in, Stay in and Tune in."

(Musak.)

The area around Paddington Station is being sealed off. All transport to and from West 2 will be stopped. Anyone within the area, is advised to remain indoors until further investigation.

CALUM: (*Getting dressed*) Can I borrow some underpants and a jacket?

RADIO: Shares are up point two and the weather continues showery.

Jess goes to fetch them.

JOHN: Who's? No, you can't. Where are you going? You can't go out. Didn't you hear what it said? Go in, stay in and tune in.

CALUM: I wonder who thought up that line?

Jess arrives with underwear and a big black waterproof jacket. Calum puts them on. He remembers his knife and tucks it into his sock.

JOHN: You can't go around with a weapon, you'll be arrested. You're not in the army any more.

CALUM: I'm just going to find out what's going on. You tune in. Remember shares are up point two.

Exit Calum. John bolts door.

JESS: Can't you two be civilized?

JOHN: Who? He's not coming back. (*Pause*) What's in that parcel anyway?

JESS: It's Luther's present.

JOHN: Open it.

JESS: Not now.

JOHN: Open it now.

JESS: No, this isn't the moment.

JOHN: It's a suspicious package. Turn the radio back on.

JESS: Why don't you take the radio upstairs to bed with you?

Exit John with radio.

CATHY: Well … Let's finish the apples.

The women peel more apples as both hum "Little Black Raincloud". Luther goes to sleep.

CATHY: Nice to see Lorry again.

JESS: If we do.

CATHY: I can't get worked-up until I know what's happening.

JESS: I wonder what Winnie the Pooh would do in a situation like this?

CATHY: He'd never have been so stupid as to leave the Hundred Acre Wood in the first place.

JESS: Stay in Eden.

CATHY: Oban. My hundred-acre wood is just outside Oban.

Cathy's beeper goes. She looks at it.

CATHY: I'm needed at the hospital.

JESS: I thought you had two days off.

CATHY: But Jess, there's an incident, as you know.

JESS: I don't want to know about it. I'm going to sit in my thinking spot and think, think, think.

CATHY: I'm sure John will keep you informed.

Cathy gets her coat.

Enter John

JOHN: Listen to this.

RADIO: (*Crackly interview with Londoner in situ*) I was standin' on a platform bit, forecourt bit, when a great big ball of flame came crashin' through the roof. A great big bang, y'know, huge bang, like a bomb. Fought it was a bomb. Ducked behind a sweet stand. 'spected to get squashed or hit, everyone on the station got down or ran behind somefing. Then there was a noise like a wind rushin' over the place and huge black horses, big as that statue in Hyde Park, wif men on 'em, except they'd black cloaks on 'em, and they were carrying some kind of weapon, like a cutting fing, over their shoulders. What a racket. I was scared. Them hooves on the platform.

REPORTER: What happened?

LONDONER: Nuffin. They just rode away across the station, out along platform 4, the Reading train, I fink.

REPORTER: Did they get on the train?

LONDONER: No, they just rode out, what a racket, these hooves, – rode away out of the station.

NEWSROOM: The nature of the explosion at Paddington Station has not been ascertained. A terrorist attack has not been ruled out. Residents in the area are advised not to go out. Go in, stay in and tune in.
Shares are down point eight and showers can be expected.

JOHN: Hear that? Shares are down already.

JESS: It's still raining.

CATHY: I'd better get to the hospital.

JESS: Sounds like there aren't many casualties.

CATHY: Orders is orders. There's lots of shock, anxiety, stress. We call them the worried well.

JOHN: Stress? What do you give them for stress?

CATHY: A nice cup of tea. You should all have one now. I'll look in later on. (*Blows kiss*).

Exit Cathy

JOHN: We'll call you.

Awkward silence. Jess puts on a kettle.

JOHN: I'll turn on the radio.

JESS: No … Don't.

JOHN: There might be some development. The explosion could've been nuclear. We need to know about Alpha and Gamma radiation; where to get duct tape, how long we need to remain indoors, that sort of thing … That fool of a brother of yours is not coming back in here unless he's been decontaminated.

JESS: Ok. Turn on the radio.

RADIO: "Continuous reporting live from the BBB *(interference which sounds like BeeBeeBeeBeeBeeBeeBee)*

John hits the radio.

RADIO: "There are as yet no reported casualties from the explosion at Paddington Station tonight. However eye-witness accounts differ.

WITNESS 1: There were definitely four huge horses, but they weren't all black, one was white …

WITNESS 2:	(*interrupting*): "… one was red …"
ANNOUNCER:	"What kind of red?"
WITNESS 3:	Bright red …
ANNOUNCER:	Some witnesses are obviously in a state of shock and St Mary's Hospital is treating people for trauma. I am now in the waiting room at the Accident and Emergency Department which is packed with patients (*Noise*) most of whom seem to have been here before the explosio … (*Noise*) … if I can just find someone … Excuse me, sir, were you present at the explosion?
WITNESS 4:	(*Accent from Indian sub-continent*) It was not an explosion, or bomb, sir. It was most definitely a fire-ball; a ball of fire from the heavens. These in my country come at times of great testing of unbelief. The goddess …
ANNOUNCER:	And here is another. Are you hurt, sir?
WITNESS 5:	No. Nobody got hurt I don't think.
ANNOUNCER:	Then why are you here?
WITNESS 5:	I'm looking for me muvver.

JESS:	He's desperately trying to find someone who got burnt!
JOHN:	I know that producer: he's an idiot.
JESS:	You think everyone's an idiot.
JOHN:	Most people are.
JESS:	Well, I disagree. They're not. Most people aren't in fact. The fault may be yours.
JOHN:	Sweetheart. You have a habit of looking at the world through rose-tinted spectacles; and that's nice. However, it's not real. Your brother for example, straight from Iraq with a suspicious package.
JESS:	He's not straight from Iraq. He went home to Oban first. The package is not from Iraq. It's Luther's present. Let's open it.
JOHN:	(*Shouts*) Don't touch it. It may be wired. I'll call the police.
JESS:	Stop over-reacting. Have this tea. (*Wry*) The police are all busy right now trying to catch some giant horses.

JOHN: That's just a cover. It's probably nuclear. Perhaps a neutron bomb.

JESS: Drink your tea.

JOHN: (*Still cross*) Don't patronize me.

JESS: I only said drink your tea.

JOHN: You're insinuating that I am being unreasonable; that I need calming down.

JESS: (*Calmly*) You do need to calm down, dear.

JOHN: "Dear"? You are being patronizing. (*Voice rising*) Don't patronize me. Don't belittle me.

JESS: I'm not … I'm trying not to.

JOHN: It's not as if I'm not a good father. I'm a very good father and I love my son.

JESS: You're a useless father. You never touch your son. You never hold him, change his nappy, feed him.

JOHN: I can't feed him.

JESS:	You never talk to him, take him out.
JOHN:	But I do feel love for him and you.
JESS:	(*Desperate*) Then do something about it. It's not enough feeling love in a vacuum. That's only half way there. Everyone feels love for someone— even monsters. Feeling love is not the same as loving. It's just not enough.

John goes over to hold Luther then stops and sits down.

JOHN:	I'm not well.
JESS:	That's how it's always been. You're a permanent invalid.
JOHN:	(*Shouting and banging the table with his hand*) Fuck you. Fuck you. Fuck you.
JESS:	You're being abusive.
JOHN:	Now you are accusing me of abuse. I've never been abusive.
JESS:	Let's all try and calm down. (*Pause*) John, I'd like to seriously consider a separation.

JOHN:	(*Shouts*) Fuck you. Fuck you. Fuck you.

Luther howls. Jess starts humming Little Black Raincloud.

The doorbell rings and Jess opens the door.

Cathy and Calum enter, faces shining.

JOHN:	What happened?
CATHY:	Nothing.
JOHN:	We know that; we listened to the radio.
CATHY:	But it's wonderful out there. It's like New Year. All the trains were stopped so the station is packed with people; but they're not angry. They're relieved. All the refreshment stalls are giving out free teas and pastries. There's no casualties.
CATHY:	Everyone's kissing each other.
JOHN:	(*Sourly*) I bet you two were.
CALUM:	(*Laughs*) You're so interested. Yes.
CALUM:	(*Takes her hand*) I've asked Cathy to marry me.

JOHN: After one free pastry. Watch out Cathy.

JESS: What did you say, Cathy?

CATHY: Yes. I said yes.

JESS: Congratulations. (*Hugging both*) I'm so glad.

JOHN: It'll end in tears.

JESS: You shut-up, John.

CATHY: So, do you recommend marriage?

John looks sheepish.

JESS: (*Strong, tearful*) We're discussing a divorce.

CATHY: (*Hugging her*) Oh Jess. I'm so glad.

JOHN: (*Shouts*) Glad? Glad?

Luther howls.

CALUM: Well, he's awake now, and we're all here. Let's open the present.

JESS: (*Glad to be distracted*) At last. Yes.

There is a lot of packing and bubble wrap. You can't see what it is from the shape. At length we see it is a huge coloured statue of the Virgin Mary carrying the infant Jesus in her arms. Her stance mirrors that of Jess with Luther. They both have serene smiles.

CALUM: I got it when I was in Bosnia.

JOHN: War Plunder.

CALUM: No. I bought it.

JOHN: We can't keep it.

JESS: Why not?

JOHN: It's offensive.

JESS: I think it's lovely, Calum. Thank you. I'll put her in Luther's room and she can watch over him.

THE END